Be a Rock

Discovering a
❯ Firm Foundation ❮
for Life

JEFFREY REYNOLDS, MD

WESTBOW
P R E S S®
A DIVISION OF THOMAS NELSON
& ZONDERVAN

Unless otherwise noted, all scripture quotations are from the ESV® Bible (The Holy Bible, English Standard Version®), copyright © 2001 by Crossway, a publishing ministry of Good News Publishers. Used by permission. All rights reserved.

Scripture quotations marked (NIV) are taken from the Holy Bible, New International Version®, NIV®. Copyright © 1973, 1978, 1984, 2011 by Biblica, Inc.™ Used by permission of Zondervan. All rights reserved worldwide. www.zondervan.com The "NIV" and "New International Version" are trademarks registered in the United States Patent and Trademark Office by Biblica, Inc.™

Scripture quotations marked CSB have been taken from the Christian Standard Bible®, Copyright © 2017 by Holman Bible Publishers. Used by permission. Christian Standard Bible® and CSB® are federally registered trademarks of Holman Bible Publishers.

This book is a work of non-fiction. Unless otherwise noted, the author and the publisher make no explicit guarantees as to the accuracy of the information contained in this book and in some cases, names of people and places have been altered to protect their privacy.

WestBow Press books may be ordered through booksellers or by contacting:

WestBow Press
A Division of Thomas Nelson & Zondervan
1663 Liberty Drive
Bloomington, IN 47403
www.westbowpress.com
1 (866) 928-1240

ISBN: 978-1-9736-5882-5 (sc)
ISBN: 978-1-9736-5884-9 (hc)
ISBN: 978-1-9736-5883-2 (e)

Library of Congress Control Number: 2019904156

Printed in the United States.

WestBow Press rev. date: 10/1/2019

Dedication

To my family, friends, colleagues, patients, and all who seek to be a rock for the benefit of others.

Table of Contents

Preface

Life in this world is inherently uncertain and unpredictable. Common sense and a little life experience make this clear to us all. Our jobs, our health, our finances, friends, marriages, and children do not come with any guarantees, at least any you can count on. While some of us may enjoy relative stability in our own personal lives, even those who are so fortunate would have to admit there are in fact problem areas, and the world we live in seems to be characterized by escalating turmoil, whether in the airwaves, in the streets, or in our own minds.

Unrest and conflict in the political, civic, economic, personal and ideological realms seems to be the new normal—especially in the U.S.A. Our senses are assaulted daily with this reality on the airwaves (TV, internet, social media). Who could fail to see that after the recent presidential election or Supreme Court hearings, as well as with virtually every other major issue of our time, regardless which side you favor? Many, it would seem, of our most valued relationships have been strained if not ruined by this ideological climate. There is also a general recognition of such rapid and important changes in our culture that, in general, people (mostly those who have been around long enough to remember the past) are becoming more alarmed, confused, or both, about the implications of these changes. I share their recognition of a profound shift in core societal values and norms since the early 60's. In the even shorter time I have been in medical practice, I have also seen an increasing proportion of people expressing or manifesting anxiety, depression and confusion, much of which I believe is a function of such changes in societal values and norms. There is also accumulating evidence of these disturbances on a societal level, as will be discussed further below.

The purpose of this book is to share how, regardless of the level of chaos, confusion and instability in our environment or in ourselves, it is possible for each of us to become a "rock" of genuine stability and substance. Doing so will enable us to live in a more noble and honorable way. Such rock-like character is inevitably accompanied by a level of internal confidence, clarity, peace and joy that is otherwise elusive. In fact, the joy and peace alone would be reason enough to take this information seriously, so great are the benefits to us. What we will be exploring is the fact that there is a rock-solid source for this stability and a basis for unfailing confidence in every area of life. This is not self-help, pop psychology, a gimmick or conventional wisdom. This is nothing less than an invitation to become a "rock" of integrity, stability and reliability for yourself and for everyone in your life. I am convinced now after many years of first-hand experience that it works — and not just for me, but for hundreds of millions of people throughout the entire world over millennia. In short, I would make a claim that may sound audacious: this may be the best and most important news you will ever hear (which you may or may not have heard before) which I am only passing along as one who has joined the ever-growing ranks of those who have discovered the same great truth which is, I am convinced, valid and applicable to everyone. And I doubt I need to convince you that having such qualities characterize your life is not only beneficial but, if you are like most of us, desperately needed — I know it certainly is for me.

I do realize that some readers may not have any concerns about their own character qualities such as have been briefly mentioned above. If you are in this category, this subject matter may not seem relevant to you on the surface, but I would urge you to consider reading on anyway, since you may still discover opportunities to become more effective in key areas of your life than you already are. My hope and prayer in writing this is that, regardless how well everything may seem to be going currently, you will consider these perspectives, and that by doing so you and those who depend on you will be positively impacted in a meaningful and long-term way.

I need to touch on my motivation and perspective for writing this book at this point. There are two major reasons why I feel compelled to do something so bold as to write about being "a rock" for yourself and for others. The first is that my own experience, which I share highlights of below, have taught me how you can (as I now understand it) have in many ways failed miserably in the past to be a "rock" in the key areas of your life, yet still be able to successfully pursue the important and, ultimately, noble goal of becoming such a "rock" in a way that will have significant and lasting impact for good for yourself and everyone you care about. The underlying and overarching truth or paradigm on which this insight is based, I have concluded, is so essential and universally applicable that I recognize my responsibility to present it openly for the benefit of all, regardless of the response I may personally receive to it. I also am sure that if this can work for me, it can work for anyone.

The second (and lesser, but still important—at least to me) reason I am writing this book is therapeutic. The discipline of putting in words what I have learned more accurately in recent years has been quite helpful in crystallizing my own understanding of this paradigm of reality. While that was not the primary motivation for this writing project, I believe the validity of the redemptive message of this book is ultimately self-evident and hopefully comes across in the following pages for your benefit. For me, getting to this point did not come easily, but it was certainly worth it, and my hope is it will be productive for you as well. One important disclaimer is this: while there is no inadequacy or flaw in the underlying truth this book is about, my ability to articulate it will be imperfect (as I am), but I am hopeful it will speak clearly to you in spite of that.

You may have heard people say about someone they know, "He's a *rock*!" or "She's *such a rock*!" which I always recognized a high form of compliment. Upon hearing such praise for another, part of me used to immediately feel convicted of my own inadequacies, yet I had no idea how to correct that core issue—but that is thankfully no longer the case. I deeply believe that if you approach this information with an open mind and a willingness to change for the better, and if you are receptive to the possibility of greater purposes for your life than you may previously have considered, then you also can come to be known as a real "rock" by those you care most about, and they in turn will be greatly blessed—and isn't that the ultimate point of life? Indeed, this type of impact for good is so powerful as to endure for generations, even down to your descendants (or those of unrelated people you will impact positively) who will never meet you. The simple fact that you are taking the time to begin reading this book indicates that you have taken a step in that journey, and I am confident if you stay with it, you will find it to have been worthwhile.

Chapter 1
Reality Check

Let's take a moment to consider the massive complexity yet remarkable order and harmony of the universe, solar system, and natural world in which we live. The level of organization and coordination seen from the infinitely large level down to the infinitesimally small, microscopic and sub-microscopic level is truly stunning. Such remarkable order is seen on a large scale, for example, in the orbiting of our planet around the sun at the perfect distance and axis of rotation to sustain life and keep a mass the size and weight of our planet on course with extreme precision indefinitely. In my premedical and medical education, I had the unusual privilege of learning quite a bit of all that modern scientific inquiry has extensively revealed of the inner workings of life from the sub-cellular and molecular scale to the cellular, organ, system, and whole organism level of human life. I was also able to get a sense in the undergraduate sciences of the incomprehensible size of the larger context in which we humans live, including the world, the solar system, galaxy and the entire universe. This educational experience, which I did later in life than usual, simply stunned me. I was frequently in awe of the undeniable majesty and wisdom represented by all such phenomena.

An important example of this at the sub-microscopic level is the energy-producing photochemical process upon which all life on this planet ultimately depends: photosynthesis. This is a remarkably ingenious and effective series of biochemical processes by which light energy from the sun drives chemical reactions in plant cells containing chlorophyll. These reactions produce both oxygen and glucose which are necessary for the existence of all animal life on this planet, while actually consuming carbon dioxide which recycles the carbon in $CO2$ (the major "greenhouse gas") into the glucose that ultimately powers all animate life.

Learning the details of this intricate process at the molecular level was an eye-opening experience for me. It was beyond and obviously far superior to anything that could have been devised by human intelligence (and in any case, we know that it wasn't). Taking these observations to an even smaller level of nature, the intricate control and order seen at the very smallest scale likewise amazed me. This includes the fact (which I learned in my premed chemistry studies) that even the infinitely tiny electrons that orbit an atom have specific orbitals they must stay within. Even more amazing, each electron (which is so small scientists are unsure if it has any mass at all) has a specific spin that occurs on an *axis* which much be maintained at all times for all life and matter to function properly. Toward the other end of scale, the massive planet Earth has a specific axis of rotation as well as an orbit that must be strictly maintained for life to exist.

How about that most common and familiar substance, water? What few people appreciate is the uniquely perfect molecular design and the resulting chemical properties of water that make all life possible and impart its unparalleled and universal cleansing power. It is impossible to overstate the simple yet sublime elegance of water in its structure and function resulting from its molecular size and shape, and most importantly the specific polarity resulting from the intentional asymmetry of the distribution of the electrons resulting from the exact arrangement of the two hydrogen atoms at precise angles relative to the central oxygen atom. This provides its unique properties and incalculable value to all living things. It donates and accepts electrons and hydrogen atoms to permit innumerable chemical reactions vital to life and provides an aqueous internal environment that makes all cellular and systemic functions possible. On top of that, there is nothing as refreshing as cold, pure water when you are thirsty, especially if you are also hot—and it has been supplied to us in great abundance for our benefit, coming up from deep in the earth and coming down from the skies to water all plant life.

Just with regard to plant life, consider the amazing diversity of plants, many of which serve as food that is not only delicious but good for you. Many plants are known for their medicinal or health properties, some of which are important staples of western medicine (with important examples being digitalis and tamoxifen). One type of plant in particular, trees, and particularly the wood which comes from them, has provided the material to make homes, boats, furniture, musical instruments, vehicles for transportation, bridges, sporting equipment, paper, boxes, and innumerable other goods—and is an ideal fuel to keep us warm and cook by! Wood's remarkable properties of tensile strength, flexibility, durability, and malleability are owed to the unique molecular structure of cellulose and the associated cell wall of that type of plant. Like the Brooklyn Bridge or the Eiffel Tower, the structure of cellulose was perfectly and ingeniously designed to enable wood to serve all these important functions for the enrichment of life and the betterment of humanity. And the icing on the cake is that most types of wood are extraordinarily beautiful in the finished product.

As remarkable as these natural phenomena are, I believe the supreme example of this principle of sublime order and superhuman genius revealed in nature at the molecular level is the structure, purpose, and function of DNA, a subject I have studied in depth at the medical school and post-doctoral research levels. When I actually grasped how DNA worked, I was in stunned awe of the undeniable level of intelligence to conceive of, and power to execute on, such a design. Most scientists seem to have had a similar epiphany when they grasped the unparalleled ingenuity of its design for the first time. The giant DNA macromolecules representing each chromosome contain millions of base pairs, which scientists were able to determine represented a form of alphabet, or code, which contains the very instructions which determine everything about your body. It is far beyond the level of genius of human alphabets and language as it is a three-dimensional form of code containing the full instructions for all the complexity of the human being—and it does so with only four "letters" based on the underlying pattern. There is a similarity to computer code, which is just a sequence of 0's and 1's, but when arranged in a certain order results in the software which runs the applications on which we all increasingly depend to live.

In an entirely different area of endeavor, but which illustrates the same truth well, is the glorious harmony, order and majesty of a great musical symphony — and to differing degrees, other kinds of music — speaks to us of a greater creative and organizing principle operating in the universe, so much so that most people find such music deeply comforting, even anxiety-relieving, in its power. Then, to point out one more example, in what is arguably the ultimate natural experience possible — having a baby — knowing that only nine months earlier it did not exist in any sense and then originated as the union of two single cells from two different people can only leave us appropriately speechless with reverent wonder at the loving intelligence and creative power that could bring this about. Even with my limited knowledge of the realm of nature and the cosmos, I could probably write volumes for the sole purpose of marveling at and celebrating this awe-inspiring process. Furthermore, in my medical practice of nephrology I am constantly reminded, through ongoing research reports as well as continuing medical education, of the staggeringly complex yet gloriously harmonious and intricate processes that are continually being discovered at the sub-cellular levels which continue to reveal the obvious genius behind it. As impressive as the technology is which has been produced by human effort and ingenuity, even the most basic processes that make living things possible—including the simplest plants—are far beyond the engineering capability of human ingenuity (as impressive as the latter admittedly is). I have noted at times throughout my medical education with wonder that many of our most brilliant scientists, some of whom have dedicated their entire lives to understanding one or a handful of such processes, remain unable to explain how these things came to be or ultimately how they are regulated at the higher levels governing such processes as DNA replication and repair, embryogenesis, or other such processes at the foundation of life itself.

〜〜〜〜〜〜〜〜〜〜〜〜〜〜〜

Now let's consider the degree of order, stability, harmony, durability and reliability of human relationships, institutions, cultural values, social norms, governments and empires. At the macro level, all the great empires and civilizations of the world have come and gone (at least in terms of their dominance or era), and it is a safe bet that those which currently exist will do likewise. Consider most governments in the world today — do they consistently live up to their mandate to make life better for the people they serve, creating the conditions for human flourishing while protecting them from every external and internal threat, or are they rather serving their own career or financial interests first and the good of the people only secondarily (or not at all)?

On a more personal level, who has never been let down, lied to, betrayed, taken advantage of, abused or rejected by a trusted friend, family member or spouse? Were our own parents all they could have, or should have, been for us? Likewise, have we ourselves been and done all we could possibly have for our spouse's and children's benefit and healthy mental, emotional, physical and spiritual growth and flourishing?

As will be clear to anyone who has lived long enough to be aware of such issues, there is an element, if not a rule, of instability in all these human systems that is characterized by such qualities as unreliability, neglect of responsibility, corruption, treachery and abuse (of power, of trust, physically, emotionally and otherwise). In addition, I have observed a growing element of or enthusiasm for anarchy or, to put it another way, lawlessness, in the world, especially today in the United States in the aftermath of the unusually strident election cycle of 2016. Life in this world is definitely not inherently bad, and there are many great blessings and joys in it, as well as—thankfully—people and factors in our lives that have been there for us and perhaps will be there for us in the future, but the point I'm making here is that, for everyone, the human experience is marked with some degree of failure, hurt, disappointment and brokenness in many, if not all, of our most important relationships and institutions. There is simply no denying or escaping this unpleasant fact of life, if we are honest with ourselves.

Increasingly, it seems most people are recognizing that, in the current era, our moral, social and economic foundations are changing, and arguably disintegrating, at an accelerating rate. This is especially apparent to those of us who live in the United States today, but is similarly true in Europe and elsewhere. There is rising contention about such fundamentals as economic policy, social policy (including such core American rights as freedom of speech and freedom of religion), immigration, international relations and other issues of the greatest importance to the world. This conflict manifests with angry, disruptive and sometimes violent "demonstrations" and rancorous talk show hosts interviewing selected people who are often all too happy to help propel this destructive process along.

But even more relevant (and ominous for society) is the increasing confusion about what can best be described as basic spiritual matters, and this clash of competing paradigms of reality has reached a fever pitch as a result of many factors, including technology that has exponentially amplified and accelerated the dissemination of ideas to the vast majority of people in the Western, and increasingly, the developing worlds. What have always been generally understood as sound precepts derived from observations of nature, moral tradition established over millennia, and common sense, are increasingly being rejected as regressive and even morally wrong by large and increasingly influential groups. The level of polarization of the major political parties or ideologies has, I believe, never been as severe as it is now, with the associated disruption of the social order and the difficulty, if not inability, to make any real progress on any of the most important challenges of our time. Such conditions have a destructive quality on people and on relationships and fosters the corruption and decay in our social norms and foundations that is already far advanced. In addition, many major countries have a level of national debt which seems to exceed sustainable or repayable levels and continues to escalate, eventually requiring austerity measures with resulting civil unrest or worse.

As if such challenges to the stability, peace and safety of society were not enough, there is a specific element operating in the world today that no one can deny is inflicting unprecedented chaos, destruction, division and fear, as well as undermining economic health and personal and religious liberty throughout the world. I am referring here to the ideologically-driven terrorism, in which the target is usually peaceful civilians minding their own business—but also those who dare to question the terrorist's actions or value set. Anyone who has felt this is not a potentially serious threat to our civil, economic and religious freedoms in the United States only need to take a good look at Europe, the Middle East and a number of northern African countries to see where things could be rapidly headed if we continue to pursue a strategy of acquiescence and appeasement to deal with it. Exhibit A in this regard for the United States is the infamous terrorist attack of September 11, 2001, in New York City, which not only was an unprecedented, unprovoked loss of civilian life on American soil, but also clearly did great harm to our economy, the effects of which are still being felt today, even as other attacks on Western values of democracy, freedom of speech and thought, and civil and religious freedoms, continue with what seems to be increasing frequency and intensity. So clearly, placing our ultimate trust in our government or the larger world economic and geopolitical system — or in our own careers, wealth, family, social connections, degrees or any worldly assets — is unwise and would ultimately result in profound disappointment. My point in bringing this particular form of global threat up at this point is only to point out the reality of the forces working against our own, and society's and the world's, well-being in the short and long run.

As potentially overwhelming as such realities can be, these factors speak mainly to the environment around us, but in our personal, emotional, economic, and private thought lives, we can identify a similar principle at work. Marriages, which serve as the foundation of the family, which in turn is the building block of society, have never seen such high rates of failure and confusion as in the current era. Many have seen their marriages — or those of our parents, siblings, children, or friends — struggle or even fail, with the resulting brokenness of the families and people involved. The failure of marriages and the resulting fragmentation of the family can be perpetuated for generations into the future. So many parents, even in intact and functional marriages, have seen their children fall into drug addiction, promiscuity or other destructive traps, as well as a pattern of underperforming, poor productivity, chronic anxiety, depression, and a lack of direction or sense of purpose for their lives. A large percentage of men turn to pornography and even infidelity to cope, which of course only further contributes to marital and family dysfunction and disintegration. I hope we can all agree that this is not a good thing. Of course, the current societal trend which stands out most with regard to the family is children being born with only one parent in their life, at least consistently—in other words, one parent not in their lives (and unfortunately it is usually the father, to be discussed further below). This is the net result of many factors, but the main one seems to be a lack of willingness of people to make a lifetime, binding commitment to each other in marriage. In my experience, people are generally recognizing that our culture is failing to honor and encourage marriage or to recognize the weighty responsibility it is to be a parent—and large percentages of children in the United States are suffering for it.

In addition, more macro factors which can undermine our stability and peace (both internal and external) and seem to be generally increasing include economic pressure, burdensome government regulations, and natural or man-made disasters. When we ourselves are hit with a significant crisis, our coping mechanisms can be overwhelmed, resulting in counterproductive or harmful ways of dealing with the pressure. The results of this real-life drama, which is the common lot of humanity to varying degrees, can render a person ineffective and without hope or a healthy vision for their future. Even worse, our personal failures can and do have far-reaching effects that can be harmful to those we care most about — and for whom we have the greatest responsibility — with effects which reach generations into the future. It should also not be overlooked that any number of scenarios, from global economic collapse to war to any other major geopolitical disruption may result in our lives being quickly and permanently altered such that all of the resources, institutions or personal capabilities on which we normally rely and which normally function may no longer do so at the time of greatest vulnerability and need. Regardless of how favorable our conditions are in this world, we can be certain of these two things: life will challenge us deeply in many ways, and at some point our natural lives will come to an end. There is no escaping these realities, no matter how hard we try to—and these truths have huge implications for how we live our lives every day.

Do you ever feel like a piece of cork on a stormy sea being tossed and bounced around, reacting to conditions and crises, without any overarching direction or purpose for your life? Are you wondering if you could possibly be devoting your life to the wrong goals and whether you are living in the most effective and beneficial way possible? If you do, you are definitely not alone. Thankfully, there is a solution to the inherently unstable and fickle nature of our lives, which is the subject of this book. With the deep stability and groundedness we will be discussing will also come a profound peace that can come no other way.

Questions for reflection:

1. Where do you see a remarkable level of order and design in life?
2. Can such order, harmony and beauty have occurred on its own or by accident?
3. Why doesn't the level of order observed in the natural sphere also characterize the realm of human activity and relationships as one might expect it to?
4. Can you cite examples from your own experience which resonate with the observation of the brokenness and dysfunctionality which pervade the human experience?

Chapter 2

The Predicament

From my professional experience as a physician, and also from observing cultural and societal trends, a number of factors are contributing to a rising epidemic of anxiety, particularly in younger people but not limited to that age group. For example, an article in the June 11, 2017 New York Times Magazine entitled "Prozac Nation is now the United States of Xanax," stated that, *"According to data from the National Institute of Mental Health, some 38 percent of girls ages 13 through 17, and 26 percent of boys, have an anxiety disorder. On college campuses, anxiety is running well ahead of depression as the most common mental health concern, according to a 2016 national study of more than 150,000 students by the Center for Collegiate Mental Health at Pennsylvania State University. Meanwhile, the number of web searches involving the term has nearly doubled over the last five years, according to Google Trends."* A study in JAMA published November 21, 2017 reported a dramatic 18.8% annual rate of increase in ED visits for self-inflicted injuries among girls aged 10-14 from 2009-2015, over which interval the rate of such self-inflicted injuries tripled, and a similar though smaller trend among females in the much larger age bracket of 10-24 over that time; while the latter statistics are not necessarily a function of anxiety or confusion specifically, it seems safe to assume that these mental/emotional conditions were likely at least a big factor in this increase. A study by the Centers for Disease Control just published January 11, 2019 in *Morbidity and Mortality Weekly Report* reports an alarming 260% increase in drug overdose deaths among women aged 30 to 64 years, from 6.7/100,000 to 24.3/100,000 population from 1999 to 2017.

The factors contributing to these trends may not be immediately obvious, but the problem is undeniable. One potential factor would be technology given the widespread utilization of devices which did not exist 20 years ago and the related changes in relationship dynamics and emotional stress. An article, *The Anxiety Epidemic,* by Dr. Larry Rosen in *Psychology Today* June 18, 2017 documents the potential role of the ubiquitous smartphone and social media technology in these developments. A JAMA Psychiatry article published September 11, 2019 which studied a cohort of 6,595 teenagers over a three-year period concluded that significant social media use was strongly associated with the later development of anxiety and depression. Teens who spent 3-6 hours per day on social media were 60% more likely to develop depression or anxiety than those who did not use social media. The effect was even larger (78%) for those who used social media more than 6 hours per day. From this and other data, as well as my own observation, it would seem that the implicit promises of technology for life enhancement may be overrated, and the downside of such activity poorly understood.

However, my sense is that changes in key societal values may be an even greater factor, particularly since the 1960's but such changes have only been accelerating more recently. In fact, it is becoming clear this country is in the throes of an ideological civil war, a reality we see demonstrated vividly every night on the cable news stations. With this underlying shift in our frame of reference, as well as the related fluidity of values which were previously more stable, the core support system of civilization—the family—disintegrating, rendering people more vulnerable to every type of stressor. And all of this is being amplified and intensified by our technology and the related social media which gives the average person little respite from these confusing and vexing pressures.

The striking prevalence of such serious psychological issues in our population, particularly within the younger demographic, points to the breakdown, or at least dysfunction, of the family in today's society. Many social scientists have documented the dramatic decline in intact families with a father and mother in a stable long-term marriage. David Blankenhorn, in his book Fatherless America, pointed out (all the way back in 1995) that "Tonight, about 40% of American children will go to sleep in homes in which their fathers do not live. Before they reach the age of 18, more than half of our nation's children are likely to spend at least a significant portion of their childhoods living apart from their fathers. Never before in this country have so many children been voluntarily abandoned by their fathers. Never before have so many children grown up without knowing what it means to have a father. Fatherlessness is the most harmful demographic trend of this generation. It is the leading cause of declining child well-being in our society. It is also the engine driving our most urgent social problems, from crime to adolescent pregnancy to child sexual abuse to domestic violence against women." [p. 1] He goes on to point out the underlying shift in cultural perspectives about the meaning, role and importance of fathers: "...as a society, we are changing our minds about the role of men in family life. As a cultural idea, our traditional understanding of fatherhood is under siege. Men in general, and fathers in particular, are increasingly viewed as superfluous to family life: either expendable or as part of the problem. Masculinity itself, understood as anything other than a rejection of what it has traditionally meant to be male, is typically treated with suspicion and even hostility in our cultural discourse. Consequently, our society is now manifestly unable to sustain, or even find reason to believe in, fatherhood as a distinctive domain of male activity." [p.2] There are of course many factors contributing to this sad reality, and examining them is not the purpose of this book, but at least recognizing that such fundamental changes have already occurred in our core societal norms and values as the family cannot be overlooked in the discussion of what it means to be a "rock" for the people in your life, especially if you are (or will some day be) a spouse or a parent.

The American family is distressed, with children in an estimated 67% of African American families being raised by only a single parent, and a very high divorce rate reportedly approaching 50% of all marriages. The most striking trend currently with regard to marriage and the family is that increasingly people are not getting married at all and do not see the advantages or reason to marry when they believe they can have the benefits of marriage without the commitment. Regardless of one's political perspective, I believe we all know that this low level of esteem for the core unit of society – marriage and the family – is setting society up for a disaster in the long run—and we are seeing societal level impact already. One example of the latter, in my estimation, is the phenomenon of criminal street gangs. The deeply ingrained human need to belong, to have a "family" with a recognized "head" is so powerful that many young people will overrule their consciences and be willing to do whatever such membership requires so they can be an accepted and trusted member of such a cohesive social unit approximating a family and headed by an authoritative male. It is no coincidence that this happens most where the dysfunction and disintegration of the family unit is most severe, such as in the inner city.

In an article by Patrick Fagan in 1999, (How Broken Families Rob Children of Their Chances For Future Prosperity; The Heritage

Foundation Backgrounder, June 11, 1999), it is noted that the single most important factor in the long-term well-being and success of children is to have both a mother and a father in an intact marriage, citing the following statistics among many others to support this assertion:

- children being reared by a single mother are 6 times more likely to live in poverty than are children of married parents.
- 73% of families with children in the bottom quintile of earnings are headed by single parents, while 95% of the highest quintile in earnings are headed by married couples.
- the problem of broken families (divorced or unmarried parents) dramatically increased from just 1950, when only 12% of children were born into a broken family, to 1992, when 58% of children were born into a broken family; and this trend has only progressed further since then.

Of all the responsibilities we are called to in life, none are greater, or more challenging, than that of marriage and parenting. Neither do other responsibilities or pursuits involve such great consequences— for good or for ill—for our lives, those of our children, and those of everyone our lives will touch, now and in the future. Yet to say that our current culture in the USA in 2017 is in a marriage and family crisis would be an understatement. All of this points to the critical need for a stabilizing, or grounding, source of truth we can turn to which will empower us to rise to the occasion and to "Be a rock" to our spouses and families. As my friend Gregory Slayton, successful venture capitalist, former diplomat, business school professor, and founder and head of a vibrant international fatherhood initiative impacting families around the world, writes in his book <u>Be A Better Dad Today</u>, "Being a good father isn't easy.... But it is absolutely the most important job you and I will ever have." (p. 13) He goes on to say that, "The fact is that children who grow up without their dads here in the United States are two to three times more likely to spend time in prison, become addicted to drugs, fail out of high school, have children themselves out of wedlock, suffer from mental illness, and die an early, violent death." (p. 13-14). So real effectiveness and success in marriage and parenting must be a top priority for those of us who are married and have children, but how well are we doing in these domains, and have we accurately assessed our performance in them?

Anyone who is not committed to remaining single permanently would, I believe, benefit greatly from noting this profound change in values and attitudes pertaining to something as critical to the well-being of people—particularly children—as marriage and the family. The likely cause-and-effect connection between this sociological disaster and the anxiety epidemic is particularly apparent among teenage girls, who are arguably the most vulnerable emotionally to the effects of such instability in the foundations of their lives. The impetus for me in recognizing the "Be a rock" paradigm is directly related to this key area of life, as for me it is in the domains of marriage and fatherhood/parenting where I have slowly come to recognize what it means to be a "rock" and how to pursue such character, substance, stability, reliability and other qualities my family needs from me and the incalculable human costs of failing to do so.

Even for those who do not seem to experience significant anxiety on a regular basis, there is increasing confusion about basic, core beliefs about how life works and especially with regard to any external, objective standard of truth. Compounding this issue is the spreading phenomenon of ideologically-driven terrorism throughout the world, which has numerous destabilizing effects on societies and compounds every other destabilizing factor we face. Then there are the escalating tensions and rhetoric between the two major political parties in the

United States, to the point of overt disruption (sometimes even violent in nature). The causes for such widespread anxiety, confusion and societal destabilization may be debatable, but the need for a stabilizing factor and a groundedness for people to live by is becoming increasingly undeniable. And while an increasingly large percentage of the population seems to be searching for meaning, direction and purpose, I likewise believe that very few are meeting with success in the quest for these most important but elusive qualities.

I think most would agree that the level of trust in the honesty, integrity and ethical conduct of our leaders in government these days is generally low and only seems to be getting worse. On a national and global level, entire countries are changing their alliances and even their governments altogether. Technology is dramatically changing and accelerating the ways people communicate, interact, and transact, with subtle but systematic effects on all our relationships, thought processes and worldview. Social media and the derivative associations are consuming an increasing portion of our time and attention and changing our approach to finding significance and meaning in our lives. People, especially in Western societies, are so influenced by their smartphones that one person or group can easily promote a new idea or standard or cause that can "go viral" and rapidly be accepted by large numbers of people who have little or no ability to properly evaluate the validity of such perspectives or information.

History also demonstrates how entire belief systems on which prior dominant civilizations were based have largely become obsolete, as in the case of the Greek deities and mythology, with such gods as Zeus, Hermes, Athena, and so on. The ancient Greeks produced the most advanced, sophisticated and impressive culture the world had seen up to their time, and this complex program of multiple deities was the very basis of their culture, yet this is no longer the case. Likewise, the Roman empire had its own pantheon of gods and goddesses, some of whom were repackaged from the Greeks, as well as the bizarre phenomenon of emperor worship, yet that also was eventually replaced by a state-sponsored form of Christianity by Constantine. While there are some folks on the fringe who still take the ancient Greek and Roman gods and goddesses seriously (and in rare cases may be gaining a following in these confused times), my point is to highlight the universally fickle nature of humanity, with people being deeply influenced by their prevailing cultures and beliefs, which are often transient and fail to stand up to the test of time.

And what about those belief systems that have endured and to which hundreds of millions or even billions adhere? In addition to Christianity, which in certain (often imperfect) forms has been the predominant belief in the west over the last perhaps 1500 years, we have Islam, Buddhism, Hinduism, Confucianism, and many smaller but distinct forms of belief which have also endured. In the past, there were significant geographical and technological barriers to the dissemination of these beliefs, but that is no longer the case. Between trans-continental air travel, television and the internet alone, virtually all barriers to exposure and advocacy for such a diverse array of beliefs have been removed. I am thankful for the ease with which I can learn instantly about any subject under the sun, but the escalation in divergent information and the increasingly apparent fact that most people simply have no way to make sense of all of it—no "true north" or reliable roadmap or paradigm by which to navigate it all, can be expected to result in rising mass confusion.

You may have heard of the "frog in the water" analogy, but it is so relevant to the discussion at this point that it's worth reviewing: A frog is placed in a large pot of cold water on a stove which is off. The frog swims around happily, and the heat is turned on. The water temperature gradually rises, and the frog does not notice because the change is gradual. When the water gets very warm, it may even feel good to the frog as it loosens up his muscles more. But before he realizes it, the water starts to boil, and he is cooked to death. If the water had been boiling to begin with when he was thrown into the pot, he would immediately have jumped out (if he could), but because the change in his environment was so gradual, he didn't notice until it was too late. I have come to see that we, as a society, are a lot like the frog in the water. Our environment has been gradually but relentlessly changing around us, but it has been so gradual and insidious that we have hardly noticed the changes, for the most part. To use another metaphor for this observation, the goalposts (representing the boundaries and values our society recognizes as acceptable or even mandatory) keep moving, and have in fact moved so far that they are not even in the vicinity of the 'field' they were originally on. If we could be people who lived in America in the 1700's and time-travelled to the present, our minds would be blown by the changes and we would immediately know we were in a very different, and much more complicated and confusing, world.

Thankfully, we do not need to be just passive victims or like mindless sheep with regard to the values and beliefs circulating around us, nor are we fatalistically determined by those ideological forces, however powerful or compelling they may seem to be. There is a way through it that leads to high and rock-solid ground—from which vantage point we can evaluate and reject or accept those values and beliefs as may be appropriate. In addition, I am going to make the case that this rock solid foundation or framework on which we can depend and operate does not change, fail or become irrelevant, regardless of the prevailing conditions around us.

How Are We Doing So Far?

Before we get to just how you and I can be a solid "rock," being firmly grounded on a foundation that remains true and reliable under all conditions and having a deep and consistent level of confidence in your ability to be a rock for others, we need to consider how our own personal experiences may illustrate this principle. Each of us will need to make a realistic and honest assessment of our own shortcomings in the areas of stability, reliability, trustworthiness, and groundedness in order to appreciate the possible need for a solution. Please consider carefully how well and how consistently you have done any of the following:

- Been a consistently respectful, obedient and helpful son or daughter to your parents, always honoring the authority they exercised in your life.
- Loved our spouses faithfully, sacrificially and unconditionally and forgiven them when they fall short or hurt us.
- Kept our promises to others, especially important ones.
- Remained sexually pure, honoring the sanctity of your current, past or future marriage.
- Avoided addictions, whether to smoking, alcohol, drugs, pornography, sex, food, gambling or otherwise.
- Repaid any debts or financial obligations we owed others — including taxes.
- Being content with our circumstances in life and refusing to envy what others may have that we do not have.
- Consistently lived with honesty and integrity, in our personal, professional, and financial lives.

I don't know about you, but an honest appraisal of these questions would probably lead most (all?) of us to conclude we have failed, to some degree and at certain times, in most or all of these important areas of life. I certainly have! Thoughtful consideration of the above items may reveal an underlying pattern of failure that is, to varying degrees, the universal lot of humanity, which some might call the "human condition." As common as such character flaws are, however, they will have destructive effects on us and those we care most about, on one level or another. An honest assessment of this reality reveals that there is a deep-rooted and seemingly intractable problem in us, which could be described as a corruption that we do not have the power or ability within ourselves to overcome or cure. If you consider the potential impact of any of the above failures by us on the people in our lives (whether past, present or future), it should be clear that the issue is serious — in fact, of paramount importance. And I suspect you intuitively know that already.

Beyond the personal level of our lives, consider the shifting ground and raging storms referenced earlier, causing fundamental cultural, spiritual, economic, demographic and geopolitical changes in the world and in our own lives. Regardless of your political, cultural or religious orientations, we can't deny that profound and sweeping change is occurring in all of these spheres of life, with at best disruptive — and at worst, catastrophic — effects on all of us. And I suspect we all would agree that this change is accelerating for a number of reasons, including but not limited to unprecedented world population, political and ideological tensions, technology, terrorism, and economic stressors.

If I have successfully made my case up to this point that our culture and even most historical civilizations and belief systems offer no durable, reliable, coherent, trustworthy or truly beneficial paradigm by which to correctly understand the world and your or my actual purpose in it (and beyond), you may be thinking, "Sure, but that's just life! That's the human condition!" There is some truth to such a response, but that is fortunately not the whole story. Such a statement implies there is no remedy for the underlying problem and that we must accept it as a given. However, while the social systems, institutions and even relationships we are counting on may be nothing more than shifting sands on which we can not depend in the long run, there is definitely a firm foundation, a larger reality, that not only does not change and is not moved based on the prevailing conditions (no matter how widely embraced) but can consistently provide all the wisdom, strength, support and guidance we need to safely and effectively navigate through all the greatest questions and most threatening storms of life. I believe there has never before in human history been a more compelling or urgent need for such a firm foundation.

Regardless of such macro considerations, however, the primary domain of concern in this book is in the personal dimension. This is because even if we are able though our talents, skills and hard work to manage our external life circumstances impeccably, there are deeper and weightier dimensions of life which will have more lasting effects, whether for good or for ill, yet tend to be neglected and misunderstood. I have learned this, so to speak, the hard way. Speaking (briefly) for myself, the many pressures and difficulties of life, both externally and internally, gradually got to me—and brought me to a point of recognition that something was fundamentally not right. Although on paper my accomplishments and circumstances may have been reasonably impressive, those more weighty concerns were suffering. As long as I focused on the former, I failed to appreciate the latter. The key elements of this process for me will be shared later in the book, but for now I would just say that it required me to be humbled and to recognize the deep brokenness involved in order to have my eyes opened to the insight I am attempting to communicate in the coming pages. Hopefully what was so profoundly difficult for me will not be nearly as difficult for you!

Questions for reflection:

1. Would you agree that there is increasing anxiety in our society today, and if so, can you cite possible reasons for that?

2. Do you have any concerns about the level of effectiveness at which you are operating in your life personally and professionally?

3. Have you felt that the values of your upbringing or culture might be either inadequate or misleading as your paradigm for life?

4. Do you think it is possible to do any better than you currently are on such metrics of life as were listed in the bullet points above?

Chapter 3
The Rock

The key to how you and I can be a "rock" for ourselves, our loved ones, colleagues and communities is to understand that a far greater "Rock" exists, upon the foundation of which we are able to become a little "rock" ourselves. Even if we could somehow be a small "rock" on our own strength and merit, unless we are attached to a much larger rock, we would still be subjected to the forces prevailing around us, not only the storms, floods and other difficulties nature sends, but to people or circumstances which can pick up and move, or even crush, a small rock that is not firmly anchored to a much larger one. To be the kind of little rock I am talking about, we need to be anchored, or solidly planted on, a far greater Rock which needs to hold fast in any storm and not change or be subject to disruption or destruction when conditions change or attacks come. Our own rock-like stability, reliability, integrity and other qualities that are critically important to a successfully lived life will not come from ourselves. Rather such capability will come from becoming founded on a far greater and infinitely stable, reliable, and trustworthy Rock.

Receiving a clear standard for how to live in the most honorable, responsible, trustworthy, loving, honest and noble way puts your own life in perspective in a way that listening to the people around you generally fails to do. Only by recognizing and understanding this for myself could I really understand the exact nature of the issues I was dealing with and appreciate the power of this truth for change and for good. Were it not for the undeniable impact this understanding has had in my life, I would not feel compelled to write about it. And I would also not bother to write this if I felt it was just another self-help method that works for me but might not work for you—it *will* work for you and for anyone else who pursues it, if they are willing to embrace this truth fully, because its applicability is universal.

The need for a stabilizing or grounding force in our lives may be illustrated by the observation that we all tend to rely on, attach to, affiliate or otherwise identify with such forces outside of us. For example, groups or causes from which we commonly derive our identity or a sense of purpose could include one's family/tribe (especially if one has highly capable or wealthy or influential parents and/or siblings); nation of residence or birth (for me, being an American, which for many is an important part of their core identity); degrees from or affiliation with prestigious academic institutions; professional/career status and affiliations; political parties or movements; civic organizations or secret societies; clubs; a social cause (as legitimate as these may be); and many other possibilities (to be enumerated further below). Some of these have definitely been a theme in my life in the past. We all naturally tend to put our confidence in, rely on, and even take great pride in such aspects of our lives. Such affiliations, credentials and involvements can also lend us a sense of significance, and we can take it so far as to make them a defining part of our identity. We may invest large amounts of time and energy in such pursuits, making them an organizing principle for our lives, and justifying such levels of involvement and commitment with the hope that they can and will provide us with a meaning, a purpose, a substance, a significance which we sense we are lacking in ourselves. But the real question is will any of these serve us well when the chips are really down, at the critical point of testing? What if there will be situations in our lives when such involvements or assets, as wonderful as they may be, can do nothing help us when our biggest crisis comes? And not just crises, but how about the worldviews, paradigms or ideologies which abound today with massive force yet may be contrary to our well-being and contrary to the truth—do we have the substance and groundedness in a correct paradigm of life and truth to withstand them? What do we do when these resources we are counting on actually fail us, when we come to recognize their limits? For example, if our marriage is failing, how will our high-powered careers, or Ivy League degrees help us? When the diagnosis comes of a terminal or potentially fatal disease, will any of these allegiances or affiliations make any meaningful difference? Ultimately, when we face our own death, what firm foundation or confidence do we have to do so? What if we find ourselves in a place (as millions did in the 20th century) where the state-mandated ideology (or more accurately, *religion*) becomes something like communism with its associated brutal form of atheism? And if we put our trust in such involvements or assets and they fail us at the point of greatest need, what might that imply about their reliability and dependability as guiding principles for our lives on a day-to-day basis when we are not in crisis mode?

At this point, a real world observation from my clinical medicine experience may be helpful. I have seen over the years numerous and frequent patients in the hospital who are completely confused, incoherent, and even sometimes unresponsive to normal stimuli for no reason that can be identified medically or psychologically. In fact, this phenomenon is so common among hospitalized patients that not only is there a medical term for it, "toxic/metabolic encephalopathy," but there is even a specialty that largely exists to address this exact problem, which has been termed geriatric psychology, or, "geri-psych" for short. While the latter specialty and the phenomenon I'm describing are on the one hand a legitimate and needed specialty (which deals with more than just this issue) and a genuine medical problem that does need to be addressed, I believe that in many cases, and I would venture to say this may be the case in the majority of such cases, these patients are demonstrating the principles I'm writing about here, in that they do not have the internal reserves (mental, emotional and of the will) to cope effectively with the stress of prolonged hospitalization. This is most commonly seen in the elderly and those who have been otherwise compromised physically or neurologically (such as by past stroke, or with dementia). This is a serious and prevalent issue which prolongs and complicates hospital admissions and drives up the cost of medical care, hence it can not be taken lightly. But to be brutally honest as a physician, in the majority of such cases where the diagnosis of a severe mental status change with no identifiable medical explanation is deemed a "toxic-metabolic encephalopathy," the truth is that the experts making such a diagnosis are often unable to identify any specific medical explanation for it. Worse still, we are usually—at least it seems to me—powerless to ameliorate the condition, which must usually be left to run its course and hopefully resolve with time and "supportive care." There are no doubt many factors that go into this phenomenon, but whatever they are in any given case, I believe these patients would have a much better chance of coping effectively and maintaining their mental/emotional equilibrium if they were in fact grounded on the Rock that we will be talking about. My conclusion in observing this phenomenon many times over many years in many different people is that while the most competent medical specialists in this field, it seems, are generally forced to acknowledge their inability to explain this issue in most cases or to do anything to resolve it directly, I believe that most of the time this distressing problem is due mainly to a lack of internal (mental/emotional/spiritual) stabilizing resources or "reserves" needed to cope with the psychological and physiological stresses of hospitalization, especially prolonged ones. My point here is that I have a high degree of confidence that those who are firmly grounded on an unshakable Rock foundation that provides internal wholeness, knowledge, wisdom, strength, hope, faith, and an underlying state of well-being are far better prepared for stressful conditions than those who do not, and I have observed this reality many times in my career.

Unfortunately, there are temporal and functional limits to the help or stabilizing force all such natural and human resources we tend to rely on for stability are capable of providing us. Worse than that, when a really big crisis hits, one in which the systems and institutions in our lives are shaken and potentially destroyed — which can happen in a wholesale manner in a time of national or international crisis — these resources may all fail us utterly...and simultaneously. Of course, the ultimate existential crisis any of us will ever face will be our deaths, and which of these things listed above will be able to help us then? In such crises, what stabilizing influence will we have to turn to, that we can count on to be reliable at the point and in the moment of our greatest need?

What the Rock is Not

Before exploring what the Rock is and how you can cultivate the ability to be a rock by virtue of your connection to the larger Rock, let's briefly consider some of the most common means people pursue in an attempt to achieve this kind of stability and durability but that cannot ultimately serve as that Rock which we really need to weather all the storms and attacks we will face. A human being is created for a purpose, much like an arrow is created to fly straight and to hit the intended target — or to use a more modern analogy, like a rocket ship designed and programmed to reach a specific destination far away. We all need to have a purpose to get us up in the morning, work hard, abide by the laws, care and provide for our families, and endure the difficulties and afflictions which are the common lot of all humanity to varying degrees. Life is inherently difficult, and we all face an array of seemingly continuous challenges in pursuing and achieving any goal of any real significance, or at least importance to us. I do believe some people are so broken and hopeless that they have no conscious purpose or goal driving them and consequently as adults tend to be dependent on others to meet their basic needs. But the fact that such people do exist who seem to have lost any purpose for living yet continue to live only serves to illustrate this principle, since those who have no driving beliefs, purposes or goals are generally unable to accomplish anything of significance for themselves, their loved ones or others.

There is an important related phenomenon that I recognize and which has been observed about humanity by social scientists and utilized by politicians, cult leaders, business leaders and so forth since the beginning of recorded history. This phenomenon is well-known to psychologists and has been termed "groupthink." Wikipedia defines "groupthink" in the following way:

...a psychological phenomenon that occurs within a group of people in which the desire for harmony or conformity in the group results in an irrational or dysfunctional decision-making outcome. Group members try to minimize conflict and reach a consensus decision without critical evaluation of alternative viewpoints by actively suppressing dissenting viewpoints, and by isolating themselves from outside influences.

Why is it that we see a recurring theme throughout history in which people in large numbers, sometimes the majority of a nation, allow someone to lead even though they have serious reservations with aspects of their leadership, values or actions? An obvious example of this from modern history would be that of Hitler and Nazi Germany, but there are numerous examples of this phenomenon, even in ancient

29

literature. The psychological pressure of agreeing with and conforming to the thought process of a group that may be set by a single individual but which ultimately large masses of people embrace represents in many ways what is most wrong with humanity. People often follow a bad or questionable leader for a number of reasons which are almost all wrong. One such reason might be to seek to please the people around them or, conversely, not to be rejected by them. Another is the lack of a stronger value set or a belief system to which they are deeply committed and which would give them the results and courage needed to go against the prevailing ideology or conventional wisdom. A third reason I would propose for this observation would be that there may be a compelling spiritual power at work through the leader for the ideology/cause that people are so readily flocking to, such as was clearly the case (I believe) with Hitler. One final reason I would propose for groupthink would be a deep-rooted human need to identify with a greater cause that they believe to be in some way noble and perhaps even transcendent.

Evidence for the proposition that all people need an overarching, motivating purpose and goal to keep going day after day, often against much hardship, is abundant when one considers the following list of the typical interests, credentials, affiliations, activities or causes:

- money/wealth/financial security
- academic degrees/intellectual elitism
- prestigious or powerful jobs/careers/important titles
- our spouses, parents or both
- our children
- social, political or ideological causes
- political power
- physical beauty, including fashion and clothing
- sports/fitness
- performing arts and fine arts

- social acceptance/popularity
- sex
- religious affiliations/involvement (this is a complex and unique subject and will be dealt with later).

What do all of these have in common? First, it needs to be noted that these activities or pursuits are not inherently bad. The problem arises in making any of these one's overarching motivation and driving purpose for our lives. Not only is there a better ultimate purpose for which we were born than these, but such pursuits all tend to appeal to our self-centered nature, our desire to keep ourselves enthroned as the ultimate master over our entire life. The problem with this is simple. Can we, in and of ourselves and without external support, be a source of wisdom, stability, reliability and provision, especially when things are going seriously wrong in our lives and the world around us? I believe the answer is evident — that we cannot. We are under the potentially fatal illusion that such things can provide us with the help, purpose and a foundation that we need to successfully navigate life. The reality is that they all fall woefully short and are utterly unable to do that for us. When the biggest tests in life come along, none of these really has the power to supply what we need most to successfully pass such tests. In fact, they will predictably fail us. In addition, none of these things, as good and potentially beneficial as some of these may be in their own right, can provide us with the ultimate sense of meaning and purpose for which we were designed and for which we live. Rather, because none of these pursuits fulfills all the higher purposes for which we were created, devotion to any of these becomes a form of enslavement.

A brief vignette of a fictional, but in real life common, scenario may be helpful here. Bob is born into an affluent family. His parents worked together to pursue the American Dream and were successful in doing so. The same value set is reinforced through both the lifestyle and the thinking of his family and his peers. He realizes that, if the highest goal of life is to be affluent, he will need to excel academically, athletically, and socially. He succeeds at these priorities and becomes wealthy. However, quite frequently he was conflicted between the pressures of his work and his responsibilities as a husband and father. He infrequently was able to attend his children's most significant events in the early years when they were young and he was building his career. Even when he was home with the children around, his mind was on his work, and to a lesser extent social activity. His conscience bothered him at times about this, but he justified it by reasoning that working hard to ensure his family's financial security would inevitably come with some costs. However, his wife eventually divorced him, mainly for infidelity, but also for being emotionally distant from her and the children. His children begin to struggle, even before they have completed school or experienced the demands of the real world, whether with drugs, poor academic performance, promiscuity or otherwise, and their relationships with him are distant and dysfunctional. With the passage of time, some aspects of his situation with his children improve, largely due to their own maturation, but his ability to positively impact their lives in the dimensions which are most significant remains poor.

I suspect we all know people whose lives have followed similar outlines. No doubt there are many factors involved in such scenarios, and I am not saying that career success is necessarily wrong or harmful. What I am saying is that making wealth acquisition (for example) the most important and guiding principle under which to organize one's life is short-sighted and will inevitably bear bad fruit. Having a correct paradigm by which to live that allows us to succeed in both the practical and personal arenas is critical.

My point here is not to be unsympathetic to the realities and pressures this fictional man faced, like the rest of us, to work hard and provide for his family, but to understand the spiritual pathology that had destructive effects on the more important people and relationships in his life and on himself. The overarching paradigm on which he established his life was wealth acquisition, but in the end, his wealth did not produce the intended results in his marriage or family, nor could it provide him with the wisdom, the faith, the vision, the courage, the peace, the stability and reliability that his family (and he himself) most needed. It is not hard to imagine that when such a character would have been faced with a morally challenging dilemma, he would have generally been either conflicted and confused about it, or simply made a decision or offered a perspective that ultimately proved counterproductive. This is a woeful state of affairs. While this vignette is admittedly a caricature of a hypothetical person's life, and such folk certainly have some level of love for their family and some degree of wisdom to provide at times, the story is meant to emphasize a principle. Though this vignette is not at all autobiographical, I can very much identify with Bob, and certainly have been around this model of worldview much of my life. The point is that no amount of degrees or professional accomplishments can make up for a lack of true groundedness on the ultimate Rock and the resulting over-emphasis on externals, to the detriment of the more important "internals" of character qualities and values, tends to lead directly to a great deal of injury and brokenness in our own lives and the lives of those we care most about.

In the environment in which I grew up, the predominant message was strong—building financial security was implicitly embraced as a life priority. On the one hand, it seems entirely rational, prudent and perhaps even admirable to devote oneself to the goal of maximizing financial security. It provides the resources and protection your family needs and in some ways maximizes opportunity for them. On the other hand, there are many drawbacks to this approach to life. For one, devoting oneself to building up a high level of financial security and independence in a world where the vast majority of people are not so fortunate tends to insulate us from the marked difficulties of day-to-day life in this world that seems to characterize the lives of most people. Such insulation tends to distance us from the sorrows and joys of our fellow human beings. While that may actually be part of the reason many pursue wealth in the first place (not that anyone would ever admit this), I would argue that this is not a healthy or wise strategy for life. Spiritually and emotionally speaking, such insulation hardens our hearts to others. Pursuing such an approach ultimately makes sense only from a self-centered perspective of life, one in which we mistakenly believe we know the formula for success and the purpose of life based on our own internal thought process. Unfortunately, operating from a self-centered mindset will render us unable to be a rock for ourselves or those to whom we are responsible.

Human beings have a deep need to recognize and adopt a higher purpose and greater goal for their lives, and a related paradigm on which to navigate the great complexity of life in this world. Actually, for most people, there are probably several components to their paradigm of life and priorities by which they live, but I believe there is usually one supremely important or overarching one (as money was in the vignette presented above) that serves as the main guiding principle or goal for their lives. This is just one very simplified scenario, but any of the interests or pursuits listed above, individually, sequentially or in combination as just noted, can readily serve as the primary driver of our motivation and the supreme principle(s) guiding our lives. And just as in the case of money, none of these can provide us with the sure foundation, the perspective, the wisdom, the faith, the hope and the love we need to operate successfully in the areas of our lives which are the most important and impactful in the long term and the grand scheme.

Perhaps you're thinking, "Well, I certainly don't rely on any of these things as a source of strength, encouragement, relief, peace, purpose or meaning!" That may perhaps be true, but I would urge you not to miss the opportunity to identify any potential areas of your life such as these which you might be allowing to have a greater influence over your thoughts and actions than is ultimately healthy. I believe the majority of us unfortunately fall into this kind of trap. One could almost say it is the "way of the world."

Even if it is, I do have good — actually, *great* — news about this issue. It does not have to be that way! We may never completely escape the influences of such factors over the course of our lives, but we can overcome them and achieve real and lasting victory over the deadly error of making any of these lesser priorities more important to us than they truly deserve to be. We can become a rock of wisdom, provision, protection, encouragement, vision, reliability and stability where such naturally compelling interests or goals have no power to undermine our effectiveness in the most critical areas of our lives. We will now turn to how this can be done.

<u>What the Rock Is</u>

There is a Rock that is reliable, faithful, trustworthy, just, and benevolent, able to provide any and all help that you could need in every situation. This may sound too good to be true, but I know from extensive personal experience and the overwhelming evidence from innumerable witnesses past and present that it is in fact not only true, but the ultimate truth on which all other truth depends. This Rock is revealed accurately and completely in a collection of ancient writings, spanning approximately 2000 years beginning around 1800-1900 B.C. As you may have guessed by now, the Rock I am alluding to is God, and the perspective I am presenting is that the writings that definitively reveal him are the found in the entirety of the Bible—and nowhere else. Before you pre-judge and discount (or shelve) this book, I believe you owe it to yourself to consider this perspective—one that is not just mine but has been revealed to large numbers of people over a long timeframe and has come be recognized by them as the ultimate truth on which everything is based.

Let's briefly consider again the natural world and universe (as touched on in the first chapter). Have you ever considered how life in its magnificent complexity came to be? Where the universe and all that is in it came from? How the sun was formed and how it somehow burns yet without being consumed for eons, endlessly (it seems) providing the massive energy and heat to make all life on the Earth possible? How something as complex and capable yet beautiful and mysterious as a human being comes into existence? Could a spontaneous, random "Big Bang" bring the universe and all matter and life into such complex and harmonious existence? Could all plant and animal life in its mind-boggling diversity, beauty and incredible functionality have come into existence as a series of random reactions of inert material? How could these events have been initiated and orchestrated? And where did that inert material even come from? I suspect most of us never seriously consider these questions and will, understandably to a certain extent, accept what the (supposedly) more learned experts tell us. However, even Charles Darwin, an agnostic (widely regarded with god-like status in academia for providing a paradigm for the appearance of all animal life (including human beings) without a Creator God), recognized that there was a power at work in nature, guiding a process which could not entirely happen on its own and without any help. When I studied undergraduate biology at Yale (on a post-baccalaureate basis for my premedical requirements), the prevailing theory being taught about the origins of life was that random elements in water were struck by lightning in such a way as to form RNA, which somehow formed DNA, which eventually managed to produce living organisms. From there, the teaching was that through stepwise changes and additions of function, life evolved from single celled organisms to the full complexity of life as we see it today, without any help from any intelligent, external power initiating or guiding the process.

I believe that honest and rational people seriously considering the prevailing scientific explanations for the development of life on this planet would recognize the implausibility of such theories, even if unable to embrace a theory of creation by a divinity. Any version of the belief that life was randomly generated, particularly on the order of complexity it exists, is in fact far less plausible than a storm sweeping through a junkyard of scrap metals and building a fully equipped Boeing 757 that can then fly itself! My point here is not as much to refute the scientists who embrace evolutionary theory as though it were a proven fact, as to point out the plausibility of the existence of a Creator who can not only create all we see, but can also redeem and provide a firm foundation for our broken lives, both in this world and for eternity. In my opinion, the main reason why people will believe a far less likely explanation for the creation than that a supernatural intelligence and power — God — actually created it all is simple: an unwillingness or inability to believe in God.

There is much in the Bible that speaks to this predicament of mankind and the need for a greater Rock to rely on — in fact, the overarching story of the Bible can be thought of in this way. People are, generally speaking, profoundly lacking in the inner resources to deal with the great trials of life, and we almost always turn to imperfect if not harmful coping mechanisms which will always fail when these greatest of all tests come along. A passage of scripture that I believe speaks most clearly to this overarching truth of life and best articulates the message of this book is the following:

"Everyone then who hears these words of mine and does them will be like a wise man who built his house on the rock. And the rain fell, and the floods came, and the winds blew and beat on that house, but it did not fall, because it had been founded on the rock. And everyone who hears

these words of mine and does not do them will be like a foolish man who built his house on the sand. And the rain fell, and the floods came, and the winds blew and beat against that house, and it fell, and great was the fall of it." (Matthew 7:24-27)

Most people who are not yet convinced of the truth of this statement may be thinking, "That's quite a grandiose claim!" — and it would be, or more accurately a false claim, unless Jesus actually is who he is presented to be in the Bible. We must all come to grips with that question: who exactly is Jesus Christ? This very question is explicitly presented by Jesus to his lead disciple, Peter, at a pivotal moment in Matthew 16:

Now when Jesus came into the district of Caesarea Philippi, he asked his disciples, "Who do people say that the Son of Man is?" And they said, "Some say John the Baptist, others say Elijah, and others Jeremiah or one of the prophets." He said to them, "But who do you say that I am?" Simon Peter replied, "You are the Christ, the Son of the living God." And Jesus answered him, "Blessed are you, Simon Bar-Jonah! For flesh and blood has not revealed this to you, but my Father who is in heaven." (Matthew 16:13-17)

The biblical perspective is that our response to the question of who Jesus really is will not only have eternal implications for you but will also have comprehensive effects on your current life. The question needs to be answered, and abstaining from (or avoiding) that determination is ultimately not going to be an option. Most of us in western countries have heard enough about him to have some opinion on him, but relatively few have taken the question seriously enough to learn what can be known about him so we can answer the question, "who do you say that I am?" correctly. For now, however, regardless of your perspective on Jesus specifically, consider what he says in the previous verses of Matthew 7:24-27. He states that hearing his words and then "doing" them has the same stabilizing and grounding effect on your life as building your "house" on a great rock would, as compared with building it on sand. Think of the house as your life. The storms in the parable refer to the various trials of life. The solid and immovable rock is the words of Jesus and obedience to them, which further implies that the ultimate Rock for us is actually Jesus, who is the only mediator between God and man (1 Tim 2:5). And it is only the contents of the Bible which can be trusted to accurately reveal him to us and to guide us once we have accepted that revelation.

The word of God, and especially the words of Jesus, are so rich and laden with truth that it may be helpful here to point out some features of the above statement which are easily overlooked, but which I believe Jesus (and the Holy Spirit speaking through him) intended to convey. Just as the "house" and the "rock" in this parable represent something real in our lives, likewise the "rain," "floods" and "winds" represent the realities we all must deal with in our own lives. Rain is a relatively gentle and gradual force of nature which often does nothing more than slowly make everything wet, but over time, due to the properties of water and the cumulative erosive and corrosive effects of the rainwater, it can destroy a house by a number of mechanisms—weakening the foundation, rotting the wood, infiltrating the roof and the walls and windows, and spreading within the structures of the house to ruin it. In our own lives, the rain could represent relatively steady and largely undramatic conditions such as a difficult marriage, ongoing financial insufficiency, chronic medical issues, a corrupt government or culture, and other such persistent conditions which may not do any obvious or immediate damage to your life but over time can be devastating. Being firmly founded and grounded on the Rock is the key to surviving such conditions, and even more importantly, enabling us to *benefit from* the afflictions as well as ultimately to change them (more on that later). Floods, on the other hand, are acute catastrophic disasters which hit you without warning and are immediately devastating to your "house"—your life—unless, of course, it is firmly anchored to the Rock. Examples of such events in our lives, including of course real floods and other natural disasters such as tsunamis, earthquakes or hurricanes, which threaten to destabilize or even destroy our lives, would include a divorce, the death of an immediate family member, a career-ending job loss, a life-threatening or terminal medical diagnosis, a bankruptcy, a military invasion or strike, and many other such major and sudden developments. Such is the very nature of our lives in this broken and fallen world that no one who has lived for very long is likely to have completely avoided such life-altering events. Again, the words of Jesus—the word of God, and in written form, the Bible—provide the only reliable foundation upon which to cope with, survive and even in the long run benefit from such adversity. Finally, the winds in the parable are a most interesting and significant detail which may be more relevant today than at any previous point in history. For purposes of this parable, the winds may represent ideologies, or perhaps more accurately, "spirits," which are moving forcefully through the world, and like natural winds, having significant visible effects on people, institutions, cultures, nations and the world. It is significant that the Greek word "*pneuma*" translated as "spirit" in the New Testament is the same word translated as "breath" or "wind" in that language. Examples from recent history of such invisible yet devastating ideological "winds" would include communism, the sexual (moral) revolution which started in the 60's, radical Islamic terrorism, and many other ideologies which move like the wind and spread their damaging effects everywhere they go. Again, the only solid foundation which would enable and empower us to stand firm and not be swept away by such "winds" threatening (and trying) to overcome and overwhelm our integrity and stability is the words of Jesus, which is by extension the word of God—in its entirety.

The scriptures report that Jesus physically ascended after his resurrection, so he is not walking on this earth the way he did during his earthly ministry (with occasional exceptions), but he left us two key and necessary resources that would teach us exactly what he had to say and wants us to know and to do—the Bible, which is available to most people in the world, especially in the west, and the Holy Spirit, which he gives to those who put their trust in him and appropriate the salvation he purchased for us on the cross. If Jesus is who he, and the Bible, say he is, then I suspect that in Matthew 7:24-27 when he says "my words" he has in view not only the actual words he spoke in his earthly ministry and were written down for us, but also all of the Bible's contents. The Bible is the very word of God which bears witness to its uniquely inspired and authoritative nature, setting it apart from any other writings, as clearly stated in 2 Timothy 3:16:

All Scripture is breathed out by God and profitable for teaching, for reproof, for correction, and for training in righteousness, that the man of God may be complete, equipped for every good work.

The biblical perspective is that the entire content of which was penned by people as they were guided to write by the Holy Spirit. In God's infinite love for mankind and by His supernatural power and for our good, He provided all that is necessary for a correct and complete (for our purposes in this life) knowledge of the truth in His written word, the Bible. While all the authors of the biblical books were by definition flawed since they were human, the Holy Spirit guided their writing such that the written product was without error. Of course, I do not expect—or advise—you to simply take my word for it, but I am challenging you to evaluate the Bible yourself and determine for yourself whether this is true. The easiest and most productive way to begin this process is, in my opinion, to carefully read at least the books of Matthew and John in the New Testament. Any one of the entire gospel accounts of Jesus' life can be read in a matter of hours, and all four gospels can be read in a few days. That, and gradually reading all of the Bible repeatedly, is exactly what I had to do to come to this conclusion, and no one could have made me believe that, nor could anyone convince me otherwise now. Since I have come to recognize this to be the case, I have come to also clearly recognize that a very significant proportion of the Christians in the world share the same perspective on the word of God and firmly believe the Bible to be the infallible, definitive, complete and final written disclosure of God's revelation to all of humanity for all time. Many readers, not only of this book but of the Bible, will reject (or even oppose) the perspective on the uniquely authoritative nature of the Bible as the only definitive written revelation of the one true and living God, but if you find yourself in that category, please consider the following.

The clear and unequivocal perspective of the Bible on itself is as I have described it above, as noted in several of the verses cited. This is very similar to the fact that Jesus Christ's perspective on himself was that he was also the very incarnation of God in the flesh, as the Son of God, and that every word He ever spoke was actually "given to me by my father in heaven," and He neither said nor did anything at all which the Father did not direct (will) him to say or do. One can either agree with this perspective or disagree with it, but like the case with the authoritativeness of the Bible as the written revelation of God, the real problem comes with the conclusion not to fully accept both perspectives. First of all, the very appearance of the Son of God in the flesh changes everything. If in fact he is the Son of God, then to disagree with anything he said is either to disagree with God himself or to reject Jesus Christ as the Son of God as revealed in the Bible. Likewise, to reject any of the biblical truths presented about the holiness and righteousness of God, the sinfulness of humanity, or the nature of sin, all the parameters for morally acceptable living (including the related standards for sexuality), the sacrificial, atoning death of Jesus Christ, his bodily resurrection from the dead, or his rule and reign eternally over all the universe, would be, by definition, to be at variance with God. So I've come to recognize the fact that, just as we ought to approach the holy, omnipotent, sovereign God of the universe with profound humility, aware of our brokenness, and in awe of his holiness and goodness toward us, it is appropriate to approach his word with the same attitude and posture. We are by nature and participation sinners who have not only fallen short of the glorious purposes of God for our lives, but have lived our lives (relative to his perfect will and purpose for us individually) as rebels, outlaws and traitors. We need to recognize that God's word is sacred, holy ground, and like Moses before the burning bush we should take off the "shoes" of our self-sufficiency, self-righteousness, and fallen humanity whenever we approach it.

A word about our sin nature is appropriate here. The Bible is clear, and my own experience has convinced me as well, that the sin issue is much deeper and more serious than I'd ever thought previously. The Bible explains how this happened in Genesis 3. The first humans, Adam and Eve, were deceived by the serpent and violated the only restriction God placed on their freedom in the garden. The effects of that were immediately catastrophic and continue to permeate life for every human being. While I cannot fully explain why this is such a deep-rooted and difficult issue, what I do know is how very real and serious a matter it is. Not only have we violated most or all of the basic minimum requirements God has rightfully placed on the human race (as crystallized in the Ten Commandments), but we have a remarkable ability to persist in this self-exalting rebellion even after we have come to a knowledge of the truth about sin and God's standards for how we are to live. The problem of sin is significantly compounded by the damage to our souls as a result of sin, whether our own or others' sin. I have come to think of the soul as our "operating system" through which we live and which characterizes us as people, including our complete personality. We are able to interact with other people and with the world and everything in it because we also have bodies that allow us to see, smell, taste, feel, move, speak, hear and do work of all types. The soul, according to the Bible, is eternal, and is generally understood as the combination of the intellect, emotions, and will. It can be seriously damaged and wounded, and consequently become deeply dysfunctional in this life. We all have been hurt, compromised and scarred to varying degrees and consequently are living and operating in a broken state whether we know it or not (and most of us don't appreciate the depth of our brokenness—I certainly hadn't until more recent years). At the very least, for starters, we are compromised in our faith in our fallen state and unable to perceive God or his Kingdom without his help—and of course the effects of this deficiency are global over our lives, at least until faith comes alive. However, our souls have been further damaged through our own and others' sins, and we are in need of healing, restoration, and often deliverance from such brokenness. In addition to this condition, in the spiritual realm there are harmful spiritual forces and even, according to the Bible, malignant spiritual beings which exploit and compound these broken, unredeemed and vulnerable areas of our souls. While this discussion may make the situation seem rather bleak, in fact it points to the need for a savior, a power and a truth that can restore our souls back to the condition for which we were created. Once we lay hold of the truth that God has in fact provided such a solution to this problem in his Son, Jesus Christ, faith and hope spring up within us, followed by restoration, healing and ultimately wholeness—providing we avail ourselves of the remarkable but specific resources God has provided for this purpose: his word, his Holy Spirit, and his people both locally and globally. Scripture inspires us to be so established on the Rock that we might become "rocks" ourselves, able to withstand the rains, floods and winds of life:

until we all attain to the unity of faith and of the knowledge of the Son of God, to mature manhood, to the measure of the stature of the fullness of Christ, so that we may no longer be children, tossed to and fro by the waves and carried about by every wind of doctrine, by human cunning, by craftiness in deceitful schemes. (Ephesians 4:13-14)

Questions for reflection:

1. What affiliations, credentials or ideologies have you attached yourself to in the past or present from which to derive a sense of identity, belonging or worth?
2. Do you think you have ever been influenced by groupthink, and if so, how can you avoid it in the future?
3. Can you identify how any "gravitational pull" from such pursuits as listed above may have been counterproductive your effectiveness and the more weighty responsibilities of your life?
4. Could a good, loving and all-powerful God exist who saw to it that we have a specific set of writings to guide us in the correct understanding of God and his will for our lives? If so, are we obliged to heed and obey it?

Chapter 4
Paradigms of Life

Everyone has, whether they are aware of it or not, constructed a paradigm of reality, or worldview, by which they operate. It may even be a patchwork of multiple paradigms which an individual simultaneously embraces. Whether people are operating totally ineffectively and in a defeated mode of helplessness or whether they are building or leading large organizations, making a fortune or garnering great fame, or anywhere between those extremes, every human being has a paradigm (or several) by which they operate. However, there can ultimately be only one correct overall paradigm of reality. No matter how fervently and passionately any one person—or many people—believe in an incorrect paradigm, it will still be incorrect. A false paradigm of life may, and often does, work in the short run with regard to a specific goal, but in the long run will be very costly on a personal (and very likely material) level and *will fail you at the point of your greatest need*. Consequently, for the sake of your own life and the lives of those who depend on or are in any way affected by your life, my appeal to you at this point is to seek and discover the one correct paradigm of reality if you have not already done so. As I have indicated, I have come to the conclusion (as hundreds of millions, if not billions, of people, also have) that the correct paradigm of reality is presented definitively in the Bible, God's written revelation and full disclosure of Himself to the world for our benefit and for His glory. My hope and plea is that you would carefully consider this perspective, or, if you are already in agreement with the broad outlines of my main thesis, to consider whether it is possible to embrace and apply this truth in a more comprehensive way in your life. To be a rock for yourself and others, in other words to operate in a consistently reliable, trustworthy and honorable manner, you need to have a correct paradigm of reality, which is why I keep pointing back to God's word, the Bible. I am fully convinced after 35 years of personal encounter with the word of God and with in-depth exposure to various alternate ways of approaching it, that there is simply no other source of the knowledge of God which compares to it. Of course there is truth found in many other sources, but it stands alone as the definitive, supreme, and only reliable primary written source of revelation of the truth which we can rely on fully.

The Rock Paradigm

The theme of God as a "Rock" and a foundation or stronghold or fortress is presented repeatedly in the ancient Hebrew scriptures of the Old Testament. Here is a small sampling of such verses:

He set my feet on a rock, giving me a firm place to stand. (Psalm 40:2b, NIV)

The Lord is my rock and my fortress and my deliverer, my God, my rock, in whom I take refuge, my shield, and the horn of my salvation, my stronghold. (Psalm 18:2)

Lead me to the rock that is higher than I, for you have been my refuge, a strong tower against the enemy. (Psalm 61:3)

He only is my rock and my salvation, my fortress; I shall not be shaken. (Psalm 62:6)

Be to me a rock of refuge, to which I may continually come; you have given the command to save me, for you are my rock and my fortress. (Psalm 71:3)

The New Testament has a number of references to God as the rock, with the most significant (in my opinion) example of this, as previously cited but repeated here due to its importance, being Matthew 7:24-27:

Everyone then who hears these words of mine and does them will be like a wise man who built his house on the rock. And the rain fell, and the floods came, and the winds blew and beat on that house, but it did not fall, because it had been founded on the rock. And everyone who hears these words of mine and does not do them will be like a foolish man who built his house on the sand. And the rain fell, and the floods came, and the winds blew and beat against that house, and it fell, and great was the fall of it.

There are many other places in the Bible where God (or his word) is referred to as a rock, but I believe the above sampling of verses suffices to demonstrate that this is a key biblical theme that has great significance for the people of God. For the ancient people of Israel, who were agrarian and keepers of livestock, often nomadic, the significance of rock as a firm, immovable foundation would be compelling, particularly as they would have been affected dramatically by the elements and natural phenomena such as the rain, winds and floods mentioned in Matthew 7:24-27. They were also, of course, subjected to droughts with resulting famines. The environmental conditions in that parable are clearly meant to be understood in both a literal (or natural) as well as metaphorical sense. For example, for the people of ancient Israel one of the most catastrophic and compelling types of "floods" they repeatedly encountered (once they were settled in the Promised Land) were the attacks and invasions of enemies such as the Philistines, Assyrians, Babylonians and others. In the time of Jesus' earthly ministry, Israel was occupied and controlled by the Roman empire, and while Rome tolerated the Jews to a degree, their freedoms were restricted and their status was subordinate to that of Roman citizens, even in their own land. As this occupation was a continuously adverse condition of life, which could have significantly corrosive effects on the people, their faith, their culture and their community over time, this could be likened to the "rain" in the parable above. On top of all that, the ancient people of Israel had to deal with the "winds" of pagan beliefs which were rampant then even as they are now. In fact, in a Roman-occupied territory such as theirs at the time, the Roman emperor was considered a deity by the people of the Roman empire of the time, to the point that refusal to worship the emperor could result in execution, as it did for many Christians in the first few centuries since Christ. In that setting, for Jesus to state that his words are the only solid and stable foundation upon which one can confidently "build" his life would be truly revolutionary—not in a political sense (as the majority of Jews at that time seem to have expected) but in a personal and spiritual one. Like so much of what he did and taught, he consistently presented bold statements of authoritative truth to his listeners, and it would be up to them to either believe or reject them—and him. Several verses, written over 2,700 years ago and about 700 years before Christ, again using the metaphor of a rock, speak strongly to this very truth about the identity and significance of Jesus Christ for the people of God:

And he will become a sanctuary and a stone of offense and a rock of stumbling to both houses of Israel, a trap and a snare to the inhabitants of Jerusalem. (Isaiah 8:14)

So this is what the Sovereign LORD says: "See, I lay a stone in Zion, a tested stone, a precious cornerstone for a sure foundation; the one who relies on it will never be stricken with panic. (Isaiah 28:16)

The great news about God's word is that it is timeless, and these verses speak to us with the same power and validity now as they did when they were first written or first read. These prophetic statements also harmonize strongly with the new testament and the gospel of

Jesus Christ. Although Jesus had huge 'rock star'-like status during his 3-year earthly ministry among large numbers of people (often thousands would be following him wherever he went), he was under attack from the moment of his birth as a result of King Herod trying to kill him when he learned prophetically that the "King of the Jews" was born, through his entire public ministry by the religious authorities of Israel at the time, until he was ultimately executed as the result of a conspiracy of the religious leaders, his betrayal by one of his 12 disciples, and God's will, to which Jesus submitted to freely and completely, knowing it would be the pivotal event for humanity in all of history and for all time. While it is well beyond the scope of this book to consider the significance of this event properly, at the very least, anyone understanding the facts of this event and the context would be able to see the unimaginable and extreme love of God for lost human beings like you and me. And the implications are not limited by time, space, culture, language, or any other environmental or situational factor.

Fidelity and Clarity of a Message

When I was younger, we got most of our favorite music by radio. In my parents' youth, before television, radio was the only means of audible mass communication by which to disemminate programming such as music, drama or comedy. In a typical urban or suburban area, a large number of radio stations are usually available on the AM and FM bands, and even more with Sirius XM (satellite) Radio. Each station represents a single point along a spectrum of almost innumerable electromagnetic wavelengths over which the programming of many stations with their discrete signals can be transmitted over great distances. So if you want to listen to classical music, you have to tune to the exact frequency which carries that programming. In the older radios I grew up with, if you wanted to hear a clear signal, you had to tune your dial to the *precise spot* on the radio spectrum where that signal is being transmitted. If you don't really know what you want to listen to, you can scan or scroll through all the stations until you find something you like, but in order to find that one station or programming you want, you will have to listen briefly to dozens of stations (as well as the static when you're not dead-center on the station on the older tuners with knobs)—and sometimes go through the entire FM or AM spectrum several times before finding what you wanted.

I have come to appreciate that the spiritual world is a lot like that radio spectrum, offering almost innumerable different explanations or ideologies for the meaning and purpose of life and how we ought to live it. The sheer array of paradigms and worldviews is confusing enough to make your head spin. To scan and sample all of these without any way to sort the truth out would be hopelessly confusing. If we are not for whatever reason able to identify and commit to one of these discrete sources of truth, we will be at the whim of our innate reactions to them, which can change just as we change our minds about anything else. If there is a source or revelation of universal and absolute truth out there, then the latter condition is to be hopelessly lost, with reference to that truth. And that is one condition we definitely do not want to be in. Hence it is of paramount importance to "dial in" to the right "station" with the information and perspective we need above all else, and to find the signal with the highest fidelity to the source.

In addition to the fidelity or accuracy of the message in question as is the point with the last analogy, another factor of great importance is the *clarity* and *strength* of that message. Much like the fidelity issue, the clarity of a message can be degraded and distorted by many factors. This is particularly the case, and I believe it is not even accidental, with the one message we most need to receive clearly. A concept from electrical engineering which is useful in this discussion is the Signal to Noise Ratio (SNR). The definition of this term is *the ratio of the strength of an electrical or other signal carrying information to that of interference, generally expressed in decibels.* (Online Dictionary) This concept was particularly important and useful during World War II at which time radio communication and radar were vitally important, and a favorable SNR was obviously critical for the successful military use of both technologies. I have come to recognize that, much like the SNR used for engineering and military purposes, the SNR concept applies to the spiritual realm, or the realm of truth and paradigms of reality, extremely well. There is an obvious application of this concept to the last technology referenced above, that of radio broadcasting, which requires having the receiver tuned to the exact wavelength on which the station is transmitting to receive a clear signal. As those of us who have been around long enough know, the higher-end radio tuners had a second dial for "fine tuning," to get it even as perfectly as possible on that sweet spot of dead center, in order to optimize the desired signal and minimize the static or "noise" that quickly degrades the signal if not exactly on the frequency on which that station transmits. The fine tuning knob moved the "needle" or frequency to which the tuner was tuned very slowly relative to the rotation of the primary tuning knob so as to easily find the exact peak of the signal, thereby minimizing the noise and maximizing the true signal.

It isn't hard to see how this principle (rather than the actual technology) applies to life in our "information age" today. There is an unprecedented and at times overwhelming amount and variety of information coming at us. Technology has brought us to the point where hardly an hour goes by without being bombarded by information through television, radio, or in the current era our smartphone or other devices capable of communicating in numerous ways and providing full and usually immediate access to the internet, with all of its websites including on-demand video of any subject or event imaginable.

Applying the *fidelity* (radio station signal) and *clarity* (signal-to-noise ratio) principles to the spiritual realm, if a true and correct paradigm has been revealed to humanity by the God of the universe, as a genuinely good and loving God might be expected to do, then there *must* be a clear and reliable "signal" that can reveal the definitive truth to us. The difficulty for us, in a world in which people have lost touch with that truth and have turned to an innumerable array of alternate explanations for how reality operates, why we are here, what the point of life is and so forth, is that there is a frankly deafening "noise" level in the spiritual realm, while the true "signal" has been muted and garbled beyond recognition by our culture. Compounding the noise and the signal degradation in the external environment, there is also for most of us (and most certainly was for me, unfortunately) a high level of internal "noise" along with confusion, self-centered carnality and unbelief preventing us from hearing the signal clearly and accurately. The task of identifying the signal and eliminating the noise is not only necessary in reference to the external environment but also to our internal environment, because our thoughts, emotions and will in our damaged state will tend to drown out whatever truth signal manages to reach our eyes or ears.

In fact, if it were a matter of random chance, the odds would be woefully poor indeed for us to discover the truth which God has revealed to the world given the cacophony of competing and alluring alternatives to that truth, compounded by our internal resistance and confusion about this most important subject matter—but, thankfully, we are not left entirely to random chance and to our own devices. The God who is the source of this one true signal actually provided to us a complete and accurate written revelation of the true "signal" with flawless clarity: the Bible. This revelation in writing has one overarching message which I have made my own imperfect attempt to summarize in the following brief statement:

There is an eternally self-existent God who created everything and is infinitely good, just, holy, powerful, merciful and loving; he created humankind in his image to live in harmonious fellowship with him, but the first humans chose to rebel against his reign and rule, and humanity has been in rebellion ever since; to reconcile us to him, he sent his own son, Jesus Christ, who was without sin, to teach us the character and will of God, to show us how God intended us to live, and to die a sacrificial, atoning death, after which he was raised from the dead and ascended to the right hand of the Father, reigning with all authority in heaven and on earth and will judge all human beings in the final judgment. He is King of kings and Lord of lords, the Alpha and the Omega, who overcomes the power of sin, of death and of the devil. No one comes to the Father except through him, and all people stand in need of the forgiveness and salvation that only he can mediate for us. He is worthy of all praise, honor and glory from all people at all times and in all places. Anything that detracts from his glory is false, and anything that gives him glory as the only Son of God and the second person of the Trinity is true.

This is obviously not the only, or the best, summary of God's basic revelation to the world, but I believe it is in harmony with the sum total of the content of the Bible, and I believe it captures the ultimate "signal" with high "fidelity" and hopefully little if any "noise." If it is true, the implications are sweeping for all of life and for all people. If it is false, this is no more than an intellectual exercise or self-indulgent fantasy. But it is one or the other.

Such a message, when heard correctly, presents a choice to those who hear it. There is a binary nature to the revelation of Christ in the flesh: believe and accept, or disbelieve and reject. Although it is fashionable today to suggest there is a third option, after much thought and study on this type of question, I am convinced such an assertion is clearly wrong and dangerously misleading. Of course you need to come to your own conclusions about this, but since the only robust and faithful accounts of the life, words and deeds of Jesus Christ are found in the gospels, I would urge you to carefully read them to evaluate the primary accounts for yourself. There is, I firmly believe, no other way to come to a solid and durable conclusion on this most important and pressing question of life.

Fortunately, God did not just interact with the ancient Israelites over a 2000 year period which ended almost 3000 years ago, and then just show up briefly (in human flesh) in the Messiah 2000 years ago. He continues to operate in our world and even in our personal lives in very real ways—sometimes even when we don't believe in him. Most of us can point to times when we somehow felt the protection or provision or mercy of God in our lives. The difficulty for most of us has been to more fully and more clearly discover the truth which is the basis for a correct paradigm of reality and the very key to life itself.

The Vein of Gold and Prevailing Paradigms

Another useful analogy borrowed from nature but also applicable to the spiritual realm and the difficult process of laying hold firmly of the unique truth from God, is the "vein of gold." As we just discussed, it is vitally important to a) find or identify the one "true" signal out of all the false ones, and b) to maximize the clarity and fidelity of that signal, which in turn involves external and internal factors. However, once one has actually done that, it is possible to "mine the deposit" of that signal, much like gold miners do when they find gold. They know that when looking for significant gold deposits, sometimes small amounts are found scattered in rock or soil, not connected to a larger deposit; but there can be found a "vein of gold" in otherwise worthless rocks which can extend a significant way and contain large amounts of high quality gold. The key to the miners' success is first to find that vein of gold and then to mine, or extract, it as completely as possible.

In the larger scheme of things, there is a huge amount of common or worthless rock out there, and a very small amount of the precious gold. Similarly, in pursuing a knowledge of the truth in the spiritual realm and the realm of life, there is a seemingly infinite amount of "spiritual" teaching out there, but if one knows what to look for and where to look, there is similarly a vein of pure spiritual gold which can be "mined" and "harvested," though never fully so as the deposit is endless in this case. This is not a theoretical point but a very practical one based on reality and my own experience, as well as that of innumerable others. Much like the wardrobe in C.S. Lewis' <u>Chronicles of Narnia</u> through which the adventurous children are able to enter into another complete world which is so great that it could never be fully explored, the Kingdom of God is accessible in this world, and is even larger and more amazing and beautiful than this visible world in which we live. However, like the back of a single wardrobe in a huge castle, finding the Kingdom of God in this world involves a persistent search and takes some work. Part of becoming and operating as a rock, we will see further below, will involve taking some steps out of our familiarity and comfort zones and into this other "world," (without ever leaving this one) which people of faith eventually come to see as every bit as real as the one we can see, feel, taste and smell in the here and now.

The key to successfully identifying and then mining that vein of gold begins with the recognition that the Bible is the word of God. Not just one source of information on that subject, but *the* definitive source. If that seems overly simplistic, just consider how complicated life is and how confusing it can be to sort out all the competing (and mutually exclusive when examined carefully) belief systems and ways of interpreting reality and life. The sheer number and variety of religious, philosophical and belief systems should be fairly obvious; consider just the largest and most significant ones in the modern era for a flavor of this situation: Christianity (with its major and minor branches resulting in a variety of expressions), Islam (which also has two major divisions as well as smaller ones), Judaism (likewise with various versions), Hinduism, Jainism, Buddhism, Taoism, Confucianism, Shintoism, Bahai, New Age, Theosophy, Wicca, secular humanism, atheism, Communism, and many others represented by smaller, though in many cases significant, numbers of people.

If one is seeking coherent or unified knowledge of the one correct truth and paradigm of reality, they will not get far by being a passive receiver of the available collective "wisdom" or prevailing beliefs. In the current era, however, a particular form of belief, or more accurately a philosophy, has arisen (or more accurately, resurfaced, as it is in actuality nothing new) to deal with this confusing and highly fragmented ideological and spiritual environment. This perspective is familiar to me personally and likely will be to you as well since it is becoming increasingly prevalent. There are multiple names or labels for this philosophy/ideological perspective. One term which describes it is *Omnism*, a belief set in which all religions or faith systems are recognized as having validity and are respected as such, in the belief that all forms of belief have truth at the core. The term was introduced by the English poet Philip J. Bailey in 1839 when he stated, "I am an omnist, and believe in all religions." An Omnist holds that all religions contain truth, that they all ultimately point to the same "god," but that no one form of religion or belief system contains complete, unique or categorical truth. While I would concede that most religions/belief systems do contain some truth to varying degrees, the major problem is with the assertion by Omnism that no one religion or belief set could have a definitive or complete version of the ultimate truth. In doing so, it rejects Christianity and the Biblical revelation. In fact, the major monotheistic world religions (Christianity, Judaism and Islam) claim precisely such a distinction of having the exclusive truth. Regardless for the moment of which, if any, belief system is actually true, I give these major religions credit for at least being honest about the fact that they generally do stipulate and require a certain exclusivity with regard to their claims on the truth. The problem with Omnism, which can also be described as the ultimate version of syncretism, is that it is based on a completely relativistic perspective on truth. It takes the view that what is true is really up to the individual. In other words the truth becomes a completely subjective matter, to be experienced and embraced as an individual. This point of view reveals a value set in which individual autonomy becomes the ultimate good and the guiding principle. Advocates of this perspective like to passionately claim that no one has a right to impose any particular set of beliefs on another. While I certainly stand strongly behind the fundamental political and civil right of people to hold to and freely express their own deeply held convictions and beliefs (as long as those beliefs do not advocate or result in obvious harm to others or any chaotic disruption of social order), such freedom does not actually validate any one belief system. To take it a step further, it is simply illogical to claim that multiple incompatible belief systems or paradigms of reality can simultaneously be correct. This would seem to be obvious, but many, and an increasing proportion of, people adamantly hold to this view. There are two serious flaws with this perspective: 1) how can multiple incompatible explanations of reality be simultaneously true? 2) If there is one correct version of the ultimate truth, why would it be wrong to share it with others once found? 3) The statement that no person has a right to *impose* beliefs on anyone else (not that any genuine Christian ever would), implies that even God does not have the right to do so! And how ludicrous is that perspective?

Another insight even more relevant to, and diagnostic of, the spiritual condition of the world today is presented by Peter Jones in his book, <u>One Or Two—Seeing a World of Difference</u>. In this book he presents an insight which clears away much of the fog about what the prevailing paradigm of life in this world really is. He describes this as "Oneism," which he describes as a worldview in which "all is one" and shares the same nature and essence, and therefore everything is "a piece of the divine." If you have heard people say that "god" is not only in everything but *is* everything, you've come across this thinking overtly. This type of theology considers all discrete forms of religious expression to have some validity (despite the problems with that presented above), but takes Omnism a step further by explicitly claiming that everything—earth, trees, animals, sun, moon, stars, us—has an inherently divine nature and that "god" is innately within all of us and all of nature. This is a massive topic and I commend you to Dr. Jones' book to explore this insight more fully, but for our current purposes, what must be noted is that in such a paradigm, there can be no God who is truly other, truly holy, and truly knowable or worthy to be worshiped. This view also implicitly legitimizes all forms of pagan and occult spirituality. It really should not even be necessary to know what the bible says to know there are huge problems with this view, which will be explored more fully later.

Interestingly, I've come to recognize that God is such a gentleman that he allows us that degree of autonomy, such that not even God is forcing us to believe in him, but in the end, if the truth is as represented in the Bible, we will find out one way or another—and it would be far better to find out while we have the chance to respond, before it's too late. The problems with Omnism include the fact that the world's two major monotheistic religions, Christianity and Islam (which collectively represent about half of the world's population) are in fact incompatible (ie, can not both be right). A superficial knowledge of these two religions should make that clear. The core, non-negotiable belief of Christianity is that Jesus Christ was the Messiah and Son of God who died for the forgiveness of our sins, making reconciliation to God possible through faith which includes recognition of his full deity as the second member of the Trinity, while for Islam, Jesus Christ was only a prophet who neither died on a cross nor was resurrected (also basic requirements of the Christian faith), further denying that he or anyone else could be a "Son of God" but rather that Muhammad is the final and definitive messenger of Allah (which is Arabic for "God") and his sayings and the related writings are the "word of Allah" which takes precedence over everything else, including the bible. Islam has its own set of beliefs and religious system that is supposed to make it possible for the Muslim to be made acceptable to God and ultimately to go to heaven after they die, but there is never any solid assurance of that in Islam, while such assurance is an integral aspect of genuine Christianity through the death of Jesus Christ on the cross. Given these simple facts about these two religions, it is clear that there is no meaningful common ground on their core beliefs. The areas of apparent agreement between them, continuing with the example, on matters such as being kind to your neighbor and putting God (or "Allah" in Islam) first, are very minor compared with the fundamental disagreement regarding the identity and deity of Jesus Christ. So the world's two largest religions turn out to be incompatible with regard to their most central doctrines.

It is therefore quite a challenge to understand how our syncretist, Omnist and Oneist friends handle this issue, but it appears that denial of facts, ignorance thereof, or both must be involved. Although it seems the average person on the street these days would at least be sympathetic to the Omnist one Oneist views of reality, most of them have not given it much serious thought, and very few have even heard such terms. My take on this observation is that the reason why most people have a belief system that is contrary to (in my opinion) obvious logical facts, yet haven't given it much thought, is that we simply do not know how to go about finding the actual truth, and even more to the point, we do not even realize we have a problem that raises the need of the solution offered by such truth. I will readily admit

I was as much in this condition as anyone until God in his infinite mercy first penetrated my unbelief and spiritual deadness 35 years ago (which I describe in more detail in Chapter 8). My experience, and the perspective of scripture, is also that even though we all have a built-in knowledge of God though the creation and by our own internal witness (or conscience), the systematic corruption of our minds and hearts in this regard prevents us from seeing this on our own and we need it to be revealed to us by God (more on that later). While our Omnist/Oneist/syncretist friends feel it is unfair and unreasonable to claim there is only one correct version of the truth, I would maintain that it is illogical and dangerous to oneself spiritually to maintain otherwise. Furthermore, how are we to possibly "hear" the "signal" coming from God if we allow the "noise" of competing—and false—ideologies and belief sets to drown it out? Does it not ultimately make sense that God would provide a clear knowledge of the one overarching, good, beautiful and glorious truth so that we could actually lay hold of that truth? God being God, he theoretically could have made it possible for humanity to have multiple options to a saving knowledge of him, but the Bible clearly presents the former solution. Jesus himself emphasized the specificity and exclusivity of the truth in the following statement in Matthew 7:13-14:

Enter by the narrow gate. For the gate is wide and the way is easy that leads to destruction, and those who enter by it are many. For the gate is narrow and the way is hard that leads to life, and those who find it are few.

This assessment of the difficulty of entering heaven may seem overstated, or as my more theologically liberal friends are fond of saying, "hyperbole." While there are arguably some minor points of somewhat hyperbolic language used by Jesus at certain points elsewhere, neither overstatement nor understatement to a degree which might in any way be misleading fits the character of Jesus or the Holy Spirit who tell only the truth and are incapable of lying, nor would either so much as distort the truth the slightest bit—especially on a Kingdom perspective of such key significance as addressed in this verse. Hence we are left with the problem of understanding what Jesus meant by saying this. The first and most important point to make about this is that the "gate" which leads to "life," the one we all want to enter, is narrow, not broad. There is a specificity and even exclusivity to the truth which is generally rejected by our culture, nor has it been well received as long as people have been around, but that makes it no less true. Should it be surprising that a truth powerful enough to redeem us from our sin nature and rebel mindset, and to grant us access to eternal life, should be specific and restrictive? I think not. To use a medical example to illustrate the power of specificity, when someone has end-stage kidney failure, they need dialysis (or a kidney transplant), not an aspirin or an antibiotic. If your car's battery is dead, putting gas in the tank will not get it to start—it needs a new battery. Similarly, the problem of our spiritual deadness and sin nature is so deep-rooted and beyond any human means to resolve it that it took such drastic and unique means as the Son of God dying on a cross to overcome all the forces preventing us from being reconciled to God and made acceptable in his sight.

What about the "broad" gate which leads to "destruction"? Could this possibly mean what it seems to, that the default path in life will lead most people to destruction, which from the larger context of scripture suggests an eternity in hell? One might try to argue that the "destruction" refers to this life, such that following the way of the world and going with the flow and the crowd would lead to destruction on the natural level. Unfortunately, simple observation of life in this world would not support that view, since the majority of people seem to get along reasonably well, and it seems overt destruction and disaster in this world is not the common experience. The other reason I believe this "destruction" term likely does not refer to this life is that the corresponding term in these verses is "life," which one could argue refers to life in this world, perhaps indicating some quality of one's life that would be enhanced or added in the here and now, but given the context I do not believe this was the intended meaning. While I do believe the latter does in fact happen for those who turn their lives over to the Lordship of Jesus Christ as discussed briefly above (such as in Isaiah 26:3 or Psalm 16:11), the way the word "life" is used in this verse seems more categorical and final than that, and a balanced reading of scripture reveals that Jesus spoke a great deal about judgment and the conditions of an eternal afterlife, repeatedly emphasizing the preeminent importance of this reality. Undoubtedly the kinds of spiritual matters Jesus is teaching us about here have application to this life, but even more to the eternal perspective. God is Spirit, and His Kingdom is not bound by time or by our natural and finite life spans, yet He remains intensely and intimately interested in our lives even now. I believe Jesus is trying to activate our faith so that we can see life, and our lives, from the same perspective which God does. And as scripture testifies in numerous places, God's perspective—the only completely correct one—is very different than our human perspective. So verses like Matthew 7:13-14 above, and John 14:6 in which Jesus clearly declares, *"I am the way and the truth and the life; no one comes to the Father except through me,"* will offend our culture's deeply pluralistic sensibilities, but the only thing that really matters in the end is what is in fact true. And God's word defines and reveals itself as the definitive truth.

The Narrow Gate

Let's consider the implications of Jesus' teaching regarding the narrow and wide gates and the hard and easy ways (as cited above in Matthew 7:13-14). The most obvious application of this principle is in the ideological or spiritual realm. In general terms, the "wide gate" and "easy way" is to go along with the opinions and perspectives of the crowd you happen to be in, whether social, political or theological. It is so easy to "go with the flow" and "not rock the boat," or "go along to get along." It is, one could say, the way of the world. Unfortunately, such an approach is generally dysfunctional, sometimes catastrophic, and rarely consistent with God's will. In the ideological and spiritual category, certainly one of the most influential and important examples of the "wide gate" and "easy way" would be in the area of pop or rock music, but our culture provides innumerable other examples of this (including the growing phenomenon of pop spirituality has also broken into the mainstream, as discussed in Chapter 5).

Many books have been written just on the subject of pop music's spiritual influence on our culture, but for illustrative purposes let's take a quick look at three particularly popular songs which were played almost incessantly on major radio stations when that was how we heard the music that was out there: Billy Joel's "Only the Good Die Young;" "Imagine" by John Lennon/The Beatles; and the Rolling Stones "Sympathy for the Devil." While the mocking and hostile mentality of these particular songs toward God is unusually blatant, the spirit behind them is entirely consistent with, and representative of, the genre of pop music or rock & roll. For example, the Joel song's protagonist taunts a girl named Virginia (obviously a reference to her virginity) with the repeated effort to persuade her to engage in premarital sex with him and lose her virginity, stating that doing so now is better than the promise of heaven later, and mocking her (in this case Catholic) religion as a waste of time, and even viewed a kind of prison. The attitude of this song is summed up in the following verse: "They say there's a heaven for those who will wait; Some say it's better but I say it ain't; I'd rather laugh with the sinners than cry with the saints; The sinners are much more fun." This perspective could arguably be excused as ignorance of the true nature of genuine "religion" or more accurately saving faith in

Jesus Christ, but the very lyrics of the song demonstrate a certain level of knowledge of the moral issues involved in sexuality and that the premarital sex he is advocating is a clear violation of God's standard and explicit command. The logic in this song is strikingly similar to the ploy of the serpent in the Garden of Eden who asked Eve, "Did God actually say, 'You shall not eat of any tree in the garden?'" (Genesis 3:1b) which when Eve responds that yes, in fact, he did, the serpent escalates to a direct attack on God's credibility and authority by saying, "You will not surely die. For God knows that when you eat of it your eyes will be opened, and you will be like God, knowing good and evil." (Genesis 3:4-5) Unfortunately, this approach worked, and it has been working ever since, as we again see demonstrated in Joel's song.

John Lennon's "Imagine" has become a virtual anthem for radical leftist ideology, resonating with communism and presenting strong atheistic sentiment in such verses as: "Imagine there's no heaven; It's easy if you try; No hell below us; Above us only sky; Imagine all the people living for today; Imagine there's no countries…nothing to kill or die for; And no religion too." On the one hand I *can* imagine these things, but what I know is that it is the nature of human beings such that those who are in power in such a world will exploit their power just as the rulers did in communist Soviet Union and other communist countries, while all the rest of the people lived in utter misery, with no incentive to build or produce or innovate, no motivation to go the extra mile or to excel in any way. Due to a fundamental lack of insight about the fallen (sin) nature of man, such a utopian global atheist/communist vision as Lennon describes in this song would, if actually implemented, only lead to a level of misery and a lack of freedom such as the world has never seen.

In the case of "Sympathy for the Devil," songwriters Keith Richards and Mick Jagger appear to be literally channeling the devil as they speak for him in the first person, with perhaps the most haughty and brazen blasphemy I believe I've encountered in all of rock music (the actual lyrics are so vile I am unwilling to put any of them on the pages of this book, but just look them up for yourself and it will be clear). Having heard the actual song many times in the past, I'd always felt it crossed a line, but only when I finally surrendered to God fully and received the Holy Spirit in a more robust way in recent years did I recognize the high level of blasphemy being expressed in this song. In fact, when the band at my wife's recent high school reunion began to play it, I had to leave the room, the evil was so palpable to me—but revealingly, it did not seem to bother anyone else from what I could tell, which I found quite troubling at the time. This leads me to the point I am trying to make here: the most troublesome and revealing fact is not that these songs were written and disseminated, but that we not only tolerate them but celebrate them, sing along with them, and dance to them. Such songs have furthermore enjoyed the highest levels of enduring popularity and sadly remain a regular staple in our culture's musical and ideological diet. The appeal of music is so powerful, its presence in our society so constant, and the group or social dynamic to fit in and go with the flow so compelling, that unless we are firmly grounded on a *solid and unchanging foundation of truth* that itself correlates with reality, we will be swept up into it—as it were, indoctrinated—along with most everyone else. While you or I may not agree with Lennon's communist or atheist sentiments, will we recognize the spirit of overt rebellion expressed in Joel's song and the seriousness of the sin involved in premarital or extramarital sex? Based on my own personal observations of the value set which was operating in my hometown, schools, and personal circumstances while I was growing up, as well as seemingly in the lives of most people in my world at that time, it would have been highly unusual, even perceived as hostile, to so much as question the near-universal practices of premarital sex or living with someone outside of marriage. This perspective was so universal that I cannot recall anyone challenging that perspective in a personal way, nor certainly did I ever do so until more recent years. Note how far the moral goalposts have been moved, a gradual process that is so insidious most people fail to recognize it, like the frog in the water. This is exactly the type of issue in view when Jesus spoke of the broad gate and easy way which leads to destruction—it takes no independent thought or resolve of the will, nor does it present any difficulty (with regard to the world around us), to give in to and embrace such a standard. On the other hand, to commit to God's standard in this particular area of moral conduct (sexuality) is a "narrow gate" and a "hard way" but it "leads to life." The Biblical standard for the gift of sexuality could not be more clear or consistent: it is meant to be used only in the context of a lifelong, monogamous, committed (in other words in marriage), heterosexual union. There is no other setting where sexual activity is acceptable or pleasing to God—and it is a serious matter in God's sight to misuse this most precious gift. Being the rock God is calling us to be involves entering that narrow gate, not the broad one leading to the way of the world.

One of the most obvious and important practical applications of the meaning of the "broad gate" and "easy way" in the current era would be undiscriminating consumption of television and Hollywood movie programming, material which vast majorities of people in our culture spend large amounts of time watching. Compounding this is the minimal amount of time people spend reading—not to mention the choice of content when we actually do read. The value set and worldview presented by such forms of entertainment is not only, for the most part, at odds with that of the Bible, it also injects a continuous outpouring (with the associated *normalization*) of vulgarity, pornography, immorality, blasphemy, disrespect and sometimes mockery of the sacred, and attitudes which are hostile to God and his reign and rule. The latter description applies to the general content of most such programming, yet there is a subset of TV shows or movies (as there is in music with such songs as discussed above) which seem to be on a mission to deconstruct and dethrone God, and these do so with an impressive level of zeal and aggressiveness. Yet many of us allow our minds to marinate in such spiritually toxic content on a daily basis, rarely if ever questioning the perspectives and attitudes presented by it. How quickly we can justify it by categorizing it as "just entertainment." It is the "wide gate" and "easy way" to indiscriminately consume the kinds of TV shows and movies which are most readily available and most popular. Of course, this principle extends to every other form of content to which we are exposed including books, Broadway shows, magazines and every other form of creative expression or information produced for mass consumption. Our current American culture has acquired a deeply ingrained optimism toward life as we currently experience it in this world, resulting in a naively permissive attitude toward the content supplied to us by Hollywood, the television industry and the music industry, along with the other options out there. We tend to have (as I certainly did in the past) a convenient policy that the typical Disney movie or prime-time TV program or chart-busting pop music was not only allowable for our children, but somehow good and healthy for them. It certainly was so much easier to take that "wide path" along with most people in our world than to have standards and be willing to encounter conflict over them for the well-being of our children. Of course I did make an effort to limit their exposure to the more flagrantly obscene material out there, but have since come to realize how poorly I did at the important parental responsibility of filtering such content when my children were young, tender and vulnerable. Most significantly, I did not adequately teach them the correct values and perspectives on such content which would have enabled them to understand the nature of the issue and make more informed and better choices on their consumption of such programming. Since I was not firmly founded on that Rock at that time—not understanding Jesus' words about the wide gate and easy way—I myself just did not have (as I've come to see it) the needed perspective on such content to prevent significant exposure to the worldliness, carnality, immorality, profanity, unbelief and the like consistently modeled in the behavior and attitudes represented in such content, in which we are immersed daily. And what you don't have, you can't give.

Consequently, if we want to become the rocks we were designed to operate as in life, it may behoove us to think again before we excuse ourselves for spending much time in front of the TV, at the movies, at rock concerts or listening to our own music indiscriminately, with the usual claim that "It's just entertainment! It's harmless!" Do we really believe that absorbing our minds in the thought processes and actions of Hollywood or TV actors, or the music icons, is totally without risk or harm? If all we know is spiritually chaotic "noise" and are unaware of any specific and transcendent "signal" from heaven of supreme value and importance through that noise, we will hear and therefore know only the noise and miss the one true signal which matters. But if we do come to recognize that heavenly "signal" from God, we should want to do all we can to minimize the noise so we can hear that signal more clearly and consistently. In this regard, while it can be quite inconvenient at times, and certainly not easy, I have made it my practice to generally avoid television and Hollywood movie programming, with occasional exceptions, mainly for the sake of relationships and to gain some exposure to what is going on in our culture. As I write these words, I am on a large jetliner, surrounded by passengers, each of whom has a video monitor with a large number of movies and television shows at their fingertips, all for free of course. My own informal survey indicates that about 2/3 of the people on this flight are watching some form of the programming being offered on this technology. Of course, not all of such programming is "bad" or in the spiritual sense demonstrably in the "noise" category, but I believe a (very) large proportion of it is. In fact, from what little of this material I have seen in recent years, and what I happen to notice on the screens all around me, most of the typical programming is of an amoral or immoral nature, with profanity, nudity, violence, sexual immorality and blasphemy being the norm. An excellent biblical word which sums up the mentality and worldview generally presented by such media is "depravity." Consider the alternative uses of the time spent in such activities, which could have been invested in reading something which would make them smarter or which could build their faith, or they could be thinking about their responsibilities and how to best honor them, or keeping a journal or doing another writing project which could be productive and beneficial to others, or for that matter serving in a volunteer capacity to meet the needs of less fortunate people, or even praying! From the perspective of our culture, it seems not to really matter how we spend our time on a long flight, or on a day off, as we categorize such time as downtime. However, the way we devote our time and attention to such activities certainly does have a formative and perspective-changing effect on our minds and hearts. Scripture speaks clearly to this truth in Romans 12 which states, *Do not be conformed to this world, but be transformed by the renewal of your mind, that by testing you may discern what is the will of God, what is good and acceptable and perfect.* (Romans 12:2) This verse clearly identifies the call of God on his people to avoid conformity to this present world and to be yielded to the renewal of our minds—with the resulting changes in our desires, what pleases us, what motivates us—submitted to the absolute reign and rule of God in our hearts, our minds and our lives.

Another verse which clearly provides a much needed reality check and a serious warning about having a casual and carefree attitude to matters of our time, our words, and our actions is the following: *"I tell you, on the day of judgment people will give account for every careless word they speak, for by your words you will be justified, and by your words you will be condemned."* (Matthew 12:36-37) While this verse deals on the surface with the words we speak, the context implies that it is not just our words but the words of others we passively tolerate/accept as well as our unspoken thoughts which will justify or convict us, because they actually reveal the content or "treasure" stored up in our hearts, as the preceding 3 verses (Matthew 12:33-35) make clear. In the same way, what we put in front of our eyes and ears, what we allow and accept without any evaluation, will reveal the condition of our hearts, which will have consequences. These are not inconsequential matters—rather, they can have profound impact on our lives and those to whom we bear responsibility. This principle applies to every major domain of life and becomes a part of the perspective we will need to cultivate if we are going to be more effective, reliable and faithful in every area of responsibility and opportunity we are presented with, more of which will be dealt with later on.

One even more basic illustration of this principle (which I do not believe was in view in this parable but serves to help make the point) would be in the dietary realm, something I've become more interested in lately. As we all know, consuming anything and everything indiscriminately which tastes good, is most available, is cheap, or is intoxicating (as with alcohol), without any restraint or discipline, will predictably lead to poor health, generally including obesity, hypertension, heart disease, diabetes, and an early death. On the other hand, wisely controlling both the quality and quantity of what you eat (assuming some basic knowledge of nutritional principles) will contribute to health, vitality and a long life. I do not think it is a coincidence that the narrow gate/wide gate principle is demonstrated through such natural categories, including in the dietary area of life. To escalate this point to one more domain of life which has far greater consequences and significance is again the area of sexuality. The wide gate and easy way would be to accept the prevailing philosophy of our culture and have sexual relations with anyone we feel like having it with, at any time. The narrow gate and hard way, by contrast, would be monogamous commitment and fidelity within the sacred boundaries of marriage between one man and one woman. The narrow gate in view here does not allow for any premarital, extramarital or even postmarital (in the case of divorce while the ex-spouse is still alive—with the possible exception of when the divorce has occurred as a result of the spouse's infidelity) sexual relations. If you are the rare person who does not view that as a narrow gate and a hard way, let me confess that I certainly do acknowledge it to be so. Only God could have a standard like that which is so very difficult and counter-cultural, but so very right and beneficial.

Even for those who do embrace this perspective and the related truth disclosures completely and without reservation, winning the war over our minds and hearts is an ongoing battle in the present world and culture. The process of "dying" to our natural, fleshly, worldly, and fallen selves will be difficult, as we seek to allow God to reign and rule in our lives and to transform our minds and our hearts, cleansing us from all unrighteousness and preparing us to be his people, walking in obedience to his will over our lives through faith. This renewal of our minds and hearts takes years of diligent pursuit and ultimately is a life-long process. However, in this process, I know from my own experience, and that of many others, that this process is more than worth it—and is even what life is ultimately about. There will also key points in our lives when there will be great breakthrough in this regard, and we will see the victory of the Holy Spirit in an important area (or stronghold) of persistent error or compromise in our lives through which the spiritual forces of darkness (evil) were able to exert their influence over our lives. At pivotal moments in our lives, if we allow God to rule in our hearts, we will experience liberation from life-long patterns of bondage in sin, hopelessness or defeat with real breakthrough in the spiritual realm, from which we are poised to take further, progressive quantum leaps. This process—sometimes episodic and sometimes much more gradual—results in new levels of renewal and freedom, while providing a progressive process of transformation from the old person dominated and often defeated by the forces which are aligned against God's will and reign in our lives, to one in which we walk in the power of God's truth and freedom from every device and distraction of the ultimate enemy of man and of God, the devil.

The role of "religion" or "the church" is a complex and large subject, but I believe our "Be A Rock" paradigm can help us in this question. Let me start by questioning the commonly expressed sentiment (often among people who profess to be believers) that "God is not interested in religion" or other similar statements. Just like the "signal-to-noise ratio" and "narrow gate/wide gate" metaphors discussed in the preceding paragraphs, it is important to define "religion" accurately. There are both faithful (or valid) and unfaithful (or invalid) forms of religious expression within the larger context of Christianity. In fact, some theologians such as John MacArthur interpret the Matthew 7:13-14 "narrow gate/wide gate" passage to be primarily referring to the church, and I would agree that the church is part of what is in view here, but I also believe it applies to life more broadly. There are churches which are passionately committed to the authority of scripture and are prepared to face hardship and persecution, if necessary, to remain faithful. On the other hand, there are increasingly many churches which have rejected the authority, accuracy and trustworthiness of scripture and embraced values from the non-Christian culture which are incompatible with scripture. The truth in this setting is relativistic and malleable, even in some of the core beliefs.

Radical Faithfulness to a Distinct Truth Proposition

What I believe God is looking for, the more I have read the Bible and grown in my relationship to him, is a genuine and radical (meaning going to the roots) faith in him through a direct and personal knowledge of Jesus Christ and his sacrificial death on the cross for our justification in him, and recognition of the Bible as the very word of God. God is not impressed or in any way manipulated by us through our religious activity, no matter how fervent. There is a great deal of magical thinking, manipulative (toward both God and the human practitioners) rules and rituals, control of peoples' minds through fear and ignorance, and other kinds of abuse done under the guise of religion which is in reality *opposed to* God's reign and rule. God is looking for people whose personal loyalty to him will be so strong and pre-eminent in their lives that everything of greatest importance to us, including religious affiliations, relationships (especially with our spouses and children), careers, and what we do with our money, will be evaluated in the light of, and subordinated to, his revealed truth. Another way to put this is that our loyalty to Christ should be so much stronger to our loyalty to any one religious form of expression or set of relationships that if there is any incompatibility or conflict between the Lord's will and these affiliations, no matter how committed or involved we may be to them, then we should be able without undue hesitation to depart from that version of religion or a counterproductive relationship out of loyalty and commitment to him, trusting in him to sort out the resulting changes. His will has to be the driving reality guiding our lives and become our will for ourselves as well—otherwise it is just lip service to call him our God. It is actually not good enough to "believe in" him, which can just be a mental exercise without any commitment; rather, we must make him Lord of our lives and submit our will to his will in everything without exception. This principle is particularly important in the area of religious affiliation. Amazingly and thankfully, the word of God presents his will for his people rather clearly and puts our lives in this world in the right perspective.

As stated by R. Russell Bixler in the introduction to Genesis in the <u>New Life Bible</u> (p.1), "The Word of God must always stand above the word of man; *we are not to judge His Word, but rather, it judges us.*" (Emphasis added.) Along the same lines and taking this perspective a bit further, the Chicago Statement on Biblical Inerrancy, produced by a panel of the most respected theologians in modern times and signed by many more, is an excellent, and in my opinion, for our purposes, definitive declaration of the Bible's authority as the uniquely revealed, complete and final written revelation of God. The summary statement at the beginning of this document is presented in the following five points:

> *1. God, who is Himself Truth and speaks truth only, has inspired Holy Scripture in order thereby to reveal Himself to lost mankind through Jesus Christ as Creator and Lord, Redeemer and Judge. Holy Scripture is God's witness to Himself. 2. Holy Scripture, being God's own Word, written by men prepared and superintended by His Spirit, is of infallible divine authority in all matters upon which it touches: it is to be believed, as God's instruction, in all that it affirms; obeyed, as God's command, in all that it requires; embraced, as God's pledge, in all that it promises. 3. The Holy Spirit, Scripture's Divine Author, both authenticates it to us by His inward witness and opens our minds to understand its meaning. 4. Being wholly and verbally God-given, Scripture is without error or fault in all its teaching, no less in what it states about God's acts in creation, about the events of world history, and about its own literary origins under God, than in its witness to God's saving grace in individual lives. 5. The authority of*

> *Scripture is inescapably impaired if this total divine inerrancy is in any way limited or disregarded, or made relative to a view of truth contrary to the Bible's own; and such lapses bring serious loss to both the individual and the Church.*

This brief statement is an excellent example of a very high signal-to-noise ratio in the domain of spiritual truth. An effective and authentic religious expression of the true historical Christian faith is likewise characterized by genuine, saving, life-giving faith (on the part of the pastors, elders, and members) that effectively and obediently addresses the central problems of life in harmony with the written revelation of God: the universal reality of sin and fallen nature of humanity; the resulting alienation from God; the need for our repentance and reconciliation to God; and the gift of regeneration unto saving faith by the Holy Spirit, resulting in new life that is abundant, eternal and marked by supernatural grace, which imparts the very qualities as have been advocated in this book, among many others.

Regarding the role of the church in serving as a stabilizing force, and a key component of the Rock upon which we must rely in our life to become a rock for ourselves and others, a few points need to be made. First of all, the Rock behind it all is always God (Father, Son and Holy Spirit), but he did institute the church, the core essence of which is the body of believers who by faith in Jesus Christ have been saved and regenerated unto new life (born again) and *their loyalty is to him above all else, including above any visible institution, even any particular church.* However, the (true) church is a special case since it is established for the sole purpose of enabling the people of God to function effectively in the world, as they come to a more accurate and more effective knowledge of God while learning to serve one another sacrificially and how to reach out to a lost and dying (both spiritually and naturally) world. The degree to which any specific church that a believer goes to can contribute to the believer's experience of becoming a rock for himself and others is the degree to which that church is fully yielded to, faithful to, and honoring of the Lord Jesus Christ above all else. This requires a recognition by the church leadership that the definitive written revelation of God is the only source text to guide God's people. The degree to which any one church body, such as any specific denomination, can do that will depend on the degree to which they are faithful to the Spirit of Jesus Christ (the Holy Spirit) and to the word of God. Anything – no matter how small or large and no matter how much enthusiasm and emphasis the church puts behind it – that is introduced into the religious experience that in any way detracts in the slightest from the glory and honor of Jesus Christ will profoundly compromise the ability of that church to serve as a rock, or more accurately to mediate the effectiveness of Christ serving as the Rock in your life. Some churches, I believe, have introduced so much error in their theology, and promulgated so many aberrant ancillary beliefs (which at best compete for our attention to the true gospel and at worst will directly undermine it) that their effectiveness to facilitate or mediate a connection for the believer with God through Jesus Christ is so compromised that a believer would be better off not attending such a church at all. I have no way to estimate what percentage of churches fall into the latter category, but it would no doubt be a very significant one. There is a particularly important section of scripture in which Jesus speaks directly to the issue of how God's people will approach and relate to him in the New Covenant:

The woman said to him, "Sir, I perceive that you are a prophet. Our fathers worshiped on this mountain, but you say that in Jerusalem is the place where people ought to worship." Jesus said to her, "Woman, believe me, the hour is coming when neither on this mountain nor in Jerusalem will you worship the Father. You worship what you do not know; we worship what we know, for salvation is from the Jews. But the hour is coming, and is now here, when the true worshipers will worship the Father in spirit and truth, for the Father is seeking such people to worship him. God is spirit, and those who worship him must worship in spirit and truth." (John 4:19-24)

These verses point out that in the future (from the vantage point of that moment), the people of God will have the ability to worship God *in spirit and truth*, no longer relying on any visible building, object, or any elaborate ritualistic forms of worship as had been the norm up to that time, and as is still the case in so much of religious expression today. While I don't believe Christ was rejecting every form of organized religion in this passage, what seems crystal clear to me is that he was underlining the importance of having a direct, personal connection to God in the spirit realm which would allow and enable them to commune with God whether they are in a church, at home, at work, in public, in a prison, at the bottom of the sea or the top of a mountain. The direct access provided to God through faith in Jesus Christ and empowered by the Holy Spirit is far more liberating, life-giving, durable, continuous, real and unrestricted than any form of organized religion could ever come close to providing. So while there is an important (and I believe essential) role for church in our lives if we are to be the people of God, the primary foundation of our lives is the words of Christ (which by extension is the totality of the Bible as suggested in the parable of Matthew 7:24-27) and the empowerment of the Holy Spirit to allow us to understand and apply the truths it reveals to our own lives specifically.

Thankfully, there are many churches that are, in this sense, radically faithful to God, but in my experience these tend to be relatively small and certainly in the minority numerically. Such churches unapologetically (yet humbly) cling to the word of God and diligently seek an accurate knowledge of God above all else through it. In this setting, that which does not line up with Scripture is to be rejected, no matter how appealing, and to go beyond Scripture in reference to the core essentials of theology will always lead to error. And error in this area of life can have catastrophic consequences.

If it sounds overly zealous to claim that the Bible is the literal word of God in writing that is valid for all times, places and people, let's take a moment to consider the alternative. On the one hand, if there really is a God who is all powerful, all wise, all good and all holy, righteous and just who had the power, wisdom and goodness to create this spectacular world and the universe we are in, then could he not also guide the creation of such a book, or collection of sacred writings, over time to provide humanity with a complete, adequate and definitive record of his will, nature and purposes for humanity? And if he did do so, would it not be right and appropriate for us, his creatures, to receive his word with joyful, childlike faith and endeavor to apply it to our lives? One verse which speaks to the kind of reverence we should have for God's word is: *But this is the one to whom I will look: he who is humble and contrite in spirit and trembles at my word.* (Isaiah 66:2b)

Now, on the other hand, consider a scenario in which we human beings, his creatures, evaluate these writings which he has provided for us, and choose to reject significant parts of them, possibly even all of them? In this case, would we not be judging God? Would we not be positioning ourselves as smarter than God? And if so, how much sense would that make? But this is exactly what I believe the majority of churches in the USA, and probably worldwide, have done with God's word. Most of the oldest and best known seminaries in the United States seem to be generally dominated by this perspective, namely, that the Bible has many serious errors and is not applicable to modern times the way it may have been when it was written. People even go so far as to claim that the perspectives in the Bible on a number of important issues are unjust, or by implication, *evil*. So if the word of God is what it bears witness to itself as being, then we have people – in fact most seminaries, pastors, theologians and religious authors – directly or indirectly presenting this very perspective. Fortunately, very large numbers of believers around the would recognize the truth of the Bible's testimony to its authoritative, divinely-inspired nature throughout, and this shared perspective provides an unparalleled platform on which God can and will advance his purposes in the world. The choice is ultimately binary in this regard: humbly and reverently accept the revealed word in this way, submitting to the will of God as he has revealed it in his word, or become the judge of scripture and therefore God – and as illogical as the latter approach is, it will be even more confusing than irrational because people will have to distance themselves from reliance on the word of God, and integrity would even mandate rejecting it entirely in that setting, but what will they replace it with? Multiculturalism and diversity? Environmentalism and Global warming? LGBTQ activism? Social justice causes such as wealth redistribution or racial inequality? The problem with the latter causes is that, apart from the proper reverence for the word of God and a recognition of its completely divinely inspired and authoritative nature, these will quickly become idols, the overarching cause upon which one builds one's life and worldview and around which we organize and prioritize our time, resources and energies. Unfortunately, as worthy as such causes may arguably be in their own right, having them become an individual's *ultimate* concern is the same situation as the man in the proverb cited above who built his house on the sand, and which was destroyed when the real storms and difficulties came against it.

We also need to be established firmly on the Rock in order to withstand the doctrines of demons and the spirit of this present age which increasingly wants to demand a total rejection of the one true God revealed in Scripture and His standards for us, especially in the area of sexuality, to embrace a spirit of lawlessness that has been growing in recent years, even in our government, and to bow to the Baal of the current age. If we were left to our own devices and were it not for the grace of God and the knowledge of God, we would no doubt do just that. But praised be God, He provides us with all the grace, wisdom, knowledge, strength, vision and resolve that we need to withstand every attack of the enemy and to even break his strongholds whenever God's will is to do so. In this world, especially in the present age, the voice of the enemy is calling us to reject God and His will for us, and to operate according to a man-centered self-will that is ultimately powered by none other than the devil himself. Again, there is really no other resource apart from that specifically provided by God for us, namely His written revelation (the Bible) and the incarnate revelation of Jesus Christ, to overcome such adverse factors. Thankfully, what God has so graciously provided is far more than sufficient to overcome and conquer everything of this world and of this present age. Even more important is to recognize that in fact Jesus Christ already did conquer these things on the cross, which was confirmed when he was raised from the dead. Those who are in Christ have are fully protected and need only to decisively lay hold of the victory that Jesus Christ has already achieved for us, which we do by faith in Him and His sacrificial death on the cross followed by His resurrection confirming all that he had said about himself, that allows us to walk in victory over all of the demonic strongholds and doctrines of demons that rule in the present age.

Questions for reflection:

1. Can you identify your own paradigm of reality? If not, why not?
2. Could there be more than one correct version of the ultimate truth regarding God and life? If not, do you believe God has actually revealed that truth to us?

3. Do you agree with the above characterization of the Bible as the ultimate "signal" from God to us, perfected in both accuracy and clarity, of the truth which humanity most needs to know?

4. How has your exposure to, and diet of information sources from the culture added to the "noise" level, contributing to a degradation of the "signal"? Do you recognize any internal "noise" in your own mind which may be preventing you from really hearing even a clear truth "signal"?

Chapter 5
Pop Spirituality and Counterfeit Rocks

The discussion of how we can be a rock would not be complete without a brief look at some of the most prevalent alternative worldviews which have been passionately championed by prominent figures and embraced by much of the public. The list is long of the colorful characters and their ideologies throughout history who have been able to tap into peoples' hearts and minds and give them a vision and purpose to which they have been willing to fully devote themselves (and often their money). Such a list would include many notable figures from history and many current public figures today in the realms of religion/spirituality, politics, the music industry, Hollywood, academia and so on. What is most pertinent for us in this regard is to learn to discern the validity, or lack thereof, of those alternate belief systems. In this chapter we will analyze some of the most prominent of these, and doing so is a necessary and important part of the process of becoming the rock you and I were created to become.

There are many factors contributing to this interesting phenomenon, not the least of which is that most people seem at times to have an unsettling awareness that something is missing or they are questioning the purpose of their life, and at such times people tend to be susceptible to sales pitches claiming to provide the answers to these deepest of questions. My goal with regard to this subject is not so much to be critical of specific people (as it could distract from the larger point), rather to examine the underlying ideologies, beliefs or spirits which they advocate, so it is unavoidable to a degree, for purposes of illustrating the hazards of embracing the teachings, doctrine, vision or leadership of such individuals, to provide just a few of the more noteworthy examples from our current culture and relate them to the larger paradigm being presented herein. Each of these examples has impacted many people, and to varying degrees our entire culture, and are worth studying briefly here as examples of false teachers/rocks.

If it seems unnecessary, or perhaps even distasteful, to confront teachings of some people who are alive today, consider the alternative of being a passive receiver of "spiritual" or other ideological teachings without any way of discerning the degree of truth and/or error contained in them. How solidly can we be grounded if that is our approach to spiritual truths? In contrast to such a directionless approach, when one begins from the biblical perspective, it will become not only possible but *necessary* to identify false spiritual and theological teachings, both for the sake of your own discernment as well as serving the function of warning others of the dangers presented by false teachings. An important aspect of being a rock ourselves is having the capability to identify and reject (for purposes of our belief set/worldview/affiliations and investments of time/money/energy) such false "rocks," since such ideologies, causes, and people will inevitably come along with remarkable regularity in our lives. And the spiritual dangers of accepting and embracing such people and their perspectives are very great to you personally, and by extension to all those you care most about.

The "Church" of Oprah

One of the most prominent examples of a highly visible public personality teaching, broadcasting and promoting certain forms of spirituality today is Oprah Winfrey. To preface my comments on this topic, let me just say that in researching her activities in this area, I came to appreciate her as a seemingly sincere and likeable person who had a very difficult, traumatic youth and is in a certain sense genuinely seeking a knowledge of the truth. She undertakes the latter by interviewing people who she (or her producers) regard as experts in spirituality. The result is an entertaining tour-de-force of an impressive number and array of such "teachers." The point of this section is not to focus on Winfrey but to examine the form(s) of spirituality she embraces and enthusiastically broadcasts with evangelical fervor to the masses who tune into her programs, but a brief look at her background is worthwhile here. She had a very unusual start in life, conceived in a random encounter between two complete strangers, which led to a very difficult situation growing up as the daughter of a single 18 year old woman. Her mother was Christian and they regularly attended the Baptist church until Oprah's teen years, but her spirituality evolved into something very different from those early roots. She has publicly recounted a key turning point for her when the pastor reportedly described God in a sermon as "a jealous God," and she related how she could not believe in any God who could be at all "jealous," as she viewed jealousy as something necessarily evil, and she turned away from the Christian faith—at least in any biblical, historic or orthodox sense—at that time. From her own testimony, she viewed this event as less of a rejection of Christianty than what she evidently now sees as a *liberation* from a "narrow-minded" Bible-based approach to God. Since then, she obviously overcame her humble roots and became one of the most successful businesswomen in history, a billionaire (net worth

$2.9 billion in 2014 according to Forbes) who runs a very lucrative and powerful media empire, a platform she is using to disseminate what has become her own approach to spirituality. While people who embrace the God and the faith revaled in and based on the Bible are generally not seduced by this approach, unfortunately millions of people clearly are being impacted. In addition, she is single-handedly turning many previously obscure teachers of this alternate spirituality into massive successes with household names and huge book sales.

Oprah has prioritized this evangelistic undertaking such that she has a TV and internet series called "Super Soul Sunday" to explore spiritual topics with a selected range of people. One such program which appears to be representative of the type of content and worldview espoused on this series was an interview with Wayne Dyer, who she effusively introduces on the show as "The father of the spiritual movement as we know it in our time." (Radio interview entitled "Peacefulness" published 9/6/13.) In her introductory comments, she glowingly describes Taoism as a very major and respected "traditional Chinese religion" which takes its name from "Tao" which literally means "The Way." Taoism, she goes on to explain, is based on the book Tao Te Ching written more than 2,500 years ago by Lao Tzu, which describes a way of living that is balanced, moral and spiritual and that works for all facets of life on earth. Dyer gave an example of how someone broke an addiction by reading the book and went on to share that his own daughter did likewise. Dyer has been so impacted by this book and philosophy/ religion that he is now fully devoted to it and wrote a book extolling the virtues of Taoism. He says that when he started researching the subject he found that most people who wrote about the Tao Te Ching concluded "it is the wisest book ever written, and the most translated book in the history of publishing—other than the Bible" (which both he and Oprah were compelled to acknowledge, it would seem, somewhat reluctantly). Dyer goes on to elaborate on the values and teachings of the book, most of which taken in isolation would be hard to disagree with. However, he makes a key point at the beginning of his comments on the book by saying, "The very first line of the book is: 'The Tao that can be named is not the Tao!'" He continues by saying, "the minute you put a label on it, it's no longer the Tao," to which Oprah replies, "Yes! I was saying this to the producer of this show, that I was thinking, 'do you need to be further evolved along the spiritual path before you can begin to accept or receive the concepts of the Tao?'" Although Dyer's response to her question was not (to his credit) to agree with Oprah's fashionable "spiritually evolved" terminology, both of them clearly embraced the idea that ultimate truth, or God, cannot be named or otherwise identified in a specific manner, as is done throughout the Bible. I do want to give Taoism credit for getting that partly right; every belief system which can be named or identified specifically is not the "way" of truth—with the one exception of Biblical truth. And the latter can most certainly be named and clearly identified with the once-for-all God-man, Jesus Christ. In fact, it is worth pausing for a moment to note that what is so powerful about the Christian faith (other than its veracity) is the supreme specificity and singularity of the name of Jesus Christ. As Philippians 2:9-11 says so well, *Therefore God has highly exalted him and bestowed on him the name that is above every name, so that at the name of Jesus every knee should bow, in heaven and on earth and under the earth, and every tongue confess that Jesus Christ is Lord, to the glory of God the Father.*

So the Tao Te Ching may be loaded with nuggets of wisdom, but on the most important point of spiritual truth it fails miserably from the Biblical perspective. It implicitly or explicitly denies that the God of the Bible (who has named himself, and who also gives his Son a name of the utmost specificity and highest possible importance for the believer) can be named and identified uniquely, so it actually negates and opposes biblical revelation.

The Secret and the "Law of Attraction"

In this interview, Dyer also brought up the book The Secret by Rhonda Byrne which has been regularly cited by Oprah as foundational for her spiritually; Dyer described the book with effusive praise and endorsed its main thesis of "The Law of Attraction" which he paraphrased as "the power of knowing that when you change the way you look at things, the things you look at change." Byrne provides a revealing summary of the purpose of the book in the introduction to her 10th Anniversary Edition in relating that in this edition, "I want to share the ten most life-changing insights I have had over the last ten years of practicing and living The Secret every day. These ten insights expand on the knowledge already contained in this book, but, if studied repeatedly and carefully practiced, they will make manifesting your desires easier than ever before, eliminate struggles and suffering, and above all will give you the opportunity to reach a level of peace and joy that you might never have felt before." (p. xi) These are some very bold claims, but apart from their implausibility, what I find most revealing from a biblical perspective is the emphasis on "your desires," "eliminating struggles and suffering," and the language that puts the self, and self-interest, at the forefront. Byrne continues in the foreword to boast how "stories of miracles began to flood in" (p. xiv) after the release of the movie based on the book, as well as "thousands of accounts of The Secret being used to bring about large sums of money and unexpected checks in the mail. People have used The Secret to manifest their perfect homes, life partners, cars, jobs, and promotions, with many accounts of businesses being transformed within days of applying The Secret." (p. xiv-xv) She ends the foreword with the promise that, "As you travel through its pages and you learn The Secret, you will come to know how you can have, be, or do anything you want." (p. xvi) The author goes on to make statements of the ultimate significance and importance of The Secret with such passages as: "The law began at the beginning of time. It has always been and will always be. It is the law that determines the complete order in the Universe, every moment of your life, and every single thing you experience in your life." (p. 5) Wow! That statement (which is representative of the message of the entire book) makes it clear that Byrne is making "The Secret" life's supreme truth, putting yourself at the center of the universe rather than the God who actually rules it, denying that we are creatures and that there is a God to whom we are accountable. The only reason she can get away with this and meet with such success purveying this false paradigm of reality is a widespread lack of the knowledge of God and our fallen nature which loves to put ourselves first and wants to *be like God*. This is exactly how the serpent in the Garden of Eden successfully tempted Eve, resulting in the fall of humanity into sin and rebellion (Genesis 3:1-7).

Amazingly, Byrne actually comes right out and states the perspective that the reader is actually *god* in many places, such as in quoting Lisa Nichols who says "You are eternal life. You are God manifested in human form, made to perfection." (p. 164) Byrne then goes on to drive this point home in saying, "You are God in a physical body. You are Spirit in the flesh. You are Eternal Life expressing itself as You. You are a cosmic being. You are all power. You are all wisdom. You are all intelligence. You are perfection. You are magnificence. You are the creator, and you are creating the creation of You on this planet." (p. 164) There could be no stronger or clearer statements which reject the actual God revealed in the Bible and the related truth about us. You don't have to have a deep knowledge of God or the Bible, however, to recognize how outrageous such statements are. Think about it—if there really is a God, how would he feel about us, his creatures, making ourselves "God" as relentlessly taught throughout The Secret? If you're not sure, the answer is: not good at all. It even reaches a truly clownish level of juvenile absurdity when, early in the book she used the analogy of Aladdin's lamp and the genie who granted him any wish (complete with a genie dramatization in the audiobook) to illustrate the point, just in case you might have missed it. (p. 45-46) The book ends with this summation statement: "The earth turns on its orbit for You. The oceans ebb and flow for you. The birds sing for You. The sun rises and it sets for You. The stars come out for You. Every beautiful thing you see, every wondrous thing you experience, is all there, for You. Take a look around. None of it can exist, without You. No matter who you thought you were, now you know the Truth of Who You Really Are. You are the master of the Universe. You are the heir to the Kingdom. You are the perfection of Life. And now you know the Secret" (p. 183)

I wouldn't have taken the time to write about this wacky and comical "self as god" paradigm if it wasn't for the fact that someone with the unparalleled influence of Winfrey has been relentlessly promoting The Secret, and the fact that it appears millions are believing it. The biggest problem with this book is it is not content to present "The Secret" as *one* important principle worth knowing, but that it is presented as *the key universal principle or truth which governs all of life*. A far more accurate title for the book would be The Lie. Not just a lie, but the lie—the same as the serpent in the Garden of Eden referenced above. While the people bringing this message (like so many other false ones) to the masses are just human vehicles for it, it must be stated clearly and recognized that the *source* of such a message is not human or natural, but demonic—it is as if the author is channeling Satan himself through this book. The serious Christian recognizes that the human beings involved in disseminating false doctrines about us and about God are not the real problem but rather are deeply lost and broken like the rest of us in our natural state apart from the grace of God. The ultimate enemies of the truth (and of God and God's people) are the spirits which are working through often well-intentioned people to undermine and negate the revealed truth and Kingdom of God. Confirming that I'm not getting a little paranoid in recognizing the demonic spiritual quality of such material, Byrne could not have made it any more obvious that this is in fact the case by placing a quote from The Emerald Tablet (c. 3000 BC) at the start of the book: "As above, so below. As within, so without." This statement, particularly the first phrase, has been a consistent hallmark or slogan of the occult and witchcraft from the beginning and is a constant signal to those who recognize its occult significance. Of course, I did not need such a clear signal of the occultic nature of this book to recognize the latter, but it certainly confirms that this is indeed the case.

Frankly, as I reflected on The Secret, I came to conclude that anyone who embraces this perspective is actually being subjected to a subtle form of psychosis to which unbridled self-interest—and rejection of God and his ultimate authority—renders them susceptible. Tellingly (in terms of underlying hypocrisy and self-serving motives behind the pop spirituality phenomenon), when Oprah asked Dyer why he declined to participate in a panel of "dignitaries" who were invited to discuss and celebrate the impact and significance of The Secret, he said he "moved on from it which I came to see as too self-centered." I appreciated his willingness to publicly object on some level to Oprah's unchecked enthusiasm for The Secret—much like he was willing to do earlier in the interview for the (frankly nauseating) concept Oprah raised of "more evolved spiritual beings"—but did Dyer recognize the seriousness and gravity of the kind of error in The Secret's approach and accordingly recant his earlier involvement and support of such a worldview when he had such a perfect opportunity to do so? I saw nothing in his comments to indicate any sense of that sentiment, but this shouldn't surprise us because in pop spirituality circles, the golden rule is you can believe whatever you want and even change what you believe, and it's all good as long as it works for *you*. What I suspect makes it possible for people like Winfrey and Dyer to suspend their powers of reason to advocate such nonsense is very simply that it sells—and sells big. Really, really big in the case of Byrne, I might add. And while Byrne was apparently raking in hundreds of millions of dollars from the book and the movie, she was engaged in several highly *un*spiritual legal wars (lawsuits) with two of the very people whose hard work over many months made her success possible and whom she had allegedly defrauded out of all the profits and most of the payments she had promised them (which would apparently have been worth some tens of millions of dollars to them). Reading their stories reveals, from the perspective of the victims, that even such "highly evolved beings" as the author of <u>The Secret</u> may have serious issues and questionable ethics. ("The Secret of Rhonda's Success," in The Australian, August 23, 2008 by Richard Guilliatt)

Oprah's Top Spiritual Thinkers Define "God"

One particularly revealing, perhaps defining, episode of Oprah's "Super Soul Sunday" was entitled, "How Do Top Spiritual Thinkers Define God?" The spiritual "experts" and their definitions of God in that show follow:

- Wayne Dyer: "It's our own divine self."
- Michael Singer: "The source of you!"
- Debbie Ford: "An energy—spiritual energy—it has no denominations, it has no judgments…"
- Devon Franklin: "He's not only the Alpha, the Omega, he's a friend, he's a confidante, he's a *buddy*, he's a lover of my soul."
- Marianne Williamson: "An all-encompassing love that is the source of all, the reality of all, and the being through which *I am.*"

- Llewellyn Vaughan-Lee: "He's my beloved, my friend, the one I look to in everything—I wouldn't try to define him because no one knows God but God. He's beyond even our own idea of the beyond!"
- Eckhart Tolle: "God is beyond all the forms of life but also indwells every form of life as their essence. God is both beyond and within."
- Gabrielle Bernstein: "The ever-present essence of love."
- Caroline Myss: "To me, God is law. God to me is mystical law because law is the nature of the universe—it is the order of things. It's universal. And the negotiating principle with mystical laws is prayer. Miracle is when God bends these laws for you."
- Iyanla Vanzant: "All that is. Everything. Breath. Life. Everything. Just get Webster's Dictionary, throw it on the floor. God is everything—not only in—but *is* everything."
- Gary Zukav: "I don't have a definition of God because I've never really understood that word. People have different understandings of it, and it's caused a great deal of conflict. If I had to say what my definition of God would be, if I were going to use that word, I would say that this universe has layers upon layers of compassion and wisdom beyond ours."
- Deepak Chopra: "God is the evolutionary impulse of the universe, God is infinite creativity, infinite love, infinite compassion, infinite caring."

I found this selection and sequence of "top spiritual thinkers" and their comments to be most significant with regard to the implications for this brand or style of spirituality. First, to be charitable, there is an element of truth in some of these comments, such as "god" being creative (although without giving him explicit credit for being the

Creator of the universe), compassionate, loving, omnipresent, and a few other qualities or attributes mentioned. However, the most consistent and striking aspect of the portrayal of God by most of these "experts" was the idea of "God" being *in everything*, such that everything is part of the substance of "God"—which used to be called "New Age" theology, now goes by other names such as "the New Spirituality" (other terms for this prevalent brand of spirituality now include "Cultural Creatives," "Integral Spiritualists," "Brights," and "Progressives.") Perhaps the most time-honored (among like-minded people) term for this worldview is the Perennial Philosophy, which is widely followed, even by such dignitaries as Prince Charles, and at the highest levels of Freemasonry. This doctrine states that we are all part of God and, taking it one short step further, *we are* "god," and this is a blanket statement that allegedly applies to all human beings equally. Nothing could be a more serious perversion of the truth. The *only* universal spiritual reality or truth which all human being can fully bank on applying to them is that we all are creatures who have no innate divinity whatsoever, and rather all have a deep-rooted sin nature that has corrupted every cell of our bodies and which is enough to break our fellowship with God until such time as we recognize this and repent of it, surrendering control of our lives to Him. *For all have sinned and fallen short of the glory of God* (Romans 3:23). *All we like sheep have gone astray; we have turned—every one—to his own way* (Isaiah 53:3). Likewise, the message of <u>The Secret</u>, like that of virtually all of Oprah's spiritual teachers, could not be more different from, and opposed to, the clear and consistent message of the Bible about the fallen, sinful, broken state of all people, and the holiness, glory and otherness of the one true God. In addition, in all of the above comments was the complete lack of specificity regarding the identity, history, deeds, character and nature of their "god", in obvious and stark contrast to the biblical presentation of a personal God who has identified and characterized himself extensively for our benefit. In fact, the only comments that had any specificity only utilized that specificity to implicitly *deny* the biblical account of who God is, particularly as in the remarks of Debbie Ford and Gary Zukov above.

There were also strong and undeniable currents of Eastern mysticism in many of the comments in which God was said to not only be *in* everything but to *be* everything. Probably not all of these "experts" would have agreed with the latter point made by a few of them, but no one seemed willing to break up the party, in that sense, by contradicting the conventional human wisdom presented in this episode. It was also a frequent theme to say that "God" is beyond knowing, far beyond anything we could begin to understand. But if that is the case, how do these people then profess to know anything about God? Doesn't the extreme lack of specificity suggest that none of them even know God *at all*? At least Gary Zukov admitted he didn't even like the word "God" because he has "never really understood that word." He even goes on to elaborate on why the idea of a specific, knowable God is so objectionable to him, then provides a pleasant and appealing sort of abstract description which in my opinion did nothing to help anyone come to a clearer sense of who God might be (and certainly lacking in accuracy). Deepak Chopra, one of the most widely read and successful (and rich) authors and speakers on spirituality (widely recognized by serious Christians for his New Age type theology) for which he can largely thank Oprah, defined God as an impersonal "force" that was "evolutionary" in character, a clever way of denying God as Creator and, by direct extension, denying the biblical account of creation which is foundational and essential to the authentic Christian and Jewish faiths. By doing so, he negates the authority and credibility of the Bible—and this is not accidental as Chopra is a very smart guy. Perhaps the most serious problem running through some of these comments was the implicit merging of the self with the concept of "god" such that there is a seamless connectedness in which we are an extension of the very substance of "god," a familiar eastern/New Age concept which denies the biblical presentation of a personal but "other," infinitely holy God who dwells in unapproachable light and in whose presence sin and imperfection can not exist. Such perspectives on the subject of "God" deny the reality of sin, of the seriousness of our broken relationship with the true and living God of the Bible, and the unique and specific solution He has provided for this problem. The Bible is clear that we do not have the capability within ourselves, no matter how hard we try, to restore right standing with God, such that God had to act in a most dramatic way that displayed the extreme extent of His love for human beings supremely in the cross, the voluntary sacrificial death of Jesus Christ, which will be discussed further. However, please do not miss the stark contrast in worldviews or paradigms of spiritual reality represented by this collection of "spiritual experts" relative to that of the Bible.

The Spiritual Supermarket of Oprah

The sheer diversity and heterogeneity of the beliefs and philosophies promoted on Oprah's shows at the very least raises the question, what does she actually believe, or think her audience should believe? In addition to the foregoing, the remarkable variety and almost chameleon-like ambiguity of the content of her shows further underscore the point: when there is no clear, distinct or singular truth proposition but instead a smorgasbord of numerous ones mixed in with the personal theories of individuals, what you end up with, at best, is a very low signal-to-noise ratio. For example, in another episode, Oprah shared how she had a spiritual breakthrough (which was not further explained) after reading Gary Zukov's <u>The Seat of the Soul</u>, particularly the chapter on "Intentions." She indicates this was the turning point for her spirituality and even her Oprah show to become "a voice for good and elevating consciousness." In one episode, she interviews Zukov, who she repeatedly describes as "one of my master teachers," and during that segment shows a portion of an interview with him from 1988 which she sees as a pivotal moment for her and others' understanding of the *soul*. He describes the soul as something much bigger than we are, that existed before we were born and will exist after we die. He also likened the soul to the "mother ship" of a fleet of ships, with us, or our personalities, being just one of the little ships in the fleet—that the soul has many personalities and we are just one of those personalities which can enter or leave the world and the body at will. Classically, in both psychological and theological thought, the soul is the essence of an individual person, and is composed of the intellect, the emotions, and the will. It is unique to who we are, even constituting who we are as we live through these three domains of our personality or personhood. We are born with it, and at death our soul is separated from the body yet remains and lives on, eternally, in the afterlife, as a distinct person (with a new and glorified body, according to the bible). Our soul remains the essence and substance of who we most truly are. So to try to say the soul is amorphous, nonspecific (to us) and only a small part of something much larger, preexisting our own lives, can neither be supported by logic, observation, or experience. However, the concept of human beings not having their own, individual soul or self is integral to Buddhism, in which the achievement of Nirvana is a result of the person's realization that he or she actually has no self or soul at all, but in fact is or becomes one with Brahman. In Hinduism, while the self or soul is not directly denied, the key principle is reincarnation by which the person has repeated opportunities to get it right, with the hope of achieving the theoretical perfection of "transcendental Brahman." So it seems that Zukov's theory of the soul represents a blend of Buddhist and Hindu thought on this subject and is by no means novel. Compared with the noble, accurate and life-giving understanding of the soul in

Judaism and Christianity, such thinking as Zukov's on a doctrine as important as the human soul is not only erroneous, but downright tiresome.

Another primary source of Oprah's inspiration, by her own admission, is the Vietnamese Buddhist monk, teacher and author, Thich Nhat Hanh, whose book <u>Living Buddha, Living Christ</u> she tells us on a Super Soul Sunday episode "never leaves my bedside." She describes him in the opening of her show on him as "one of the most influential spiritual leaders of our time." He led a peaceful protest movement in Vietnam in the 60's, was nominated for the Nobel Peace Prize, and started a monastery and retreat center in France dedicated to "mindful meditation." As he describes it in his interview with Oprah, his form of spirituality involves breathing exercises, mindfulness of the present moment, appreciation of being alive, receiving healing and enlightenment and enabling others to do likewise. At one point he says, "If you are fully present in the here and the now, you need only to make a step or take a breath in order to enter the kingdom of god." He goes on to say that happiness and inner peace is possible through these practices. Although he mentions "god," he does so in a way that is abstract and non-specific, more of a concept of the "ultimate being." I have no doubt that this seemingly good-natured and presumably sincere man is authentically living out the approach he teaches, with an admirable degree of apparent integrity in that regard. However, while this approach seems to be working well for him, and his lifestyle of discipline, simplicity and self control are in a certain sense impressive, there is something flagrantly ironic in the spectacle of an American multi-billionaire media giant, described as "the Queen of All Media," running a vast money-making empire, to be seeking spiritual wisdom from a voluntarily and permanently celibate and impoverished Vietnamese Buddhist monk whose life could not be more different from hers—and from most of her viewers. Can someone who is so rich, powerful, famous, and extremely busy in general (as well as married!) really apprehend and apply the teachings of someone who has paid the personal price of lifelong poverty, celibacy/singleness and a lifestyle of unhurried, quiet contemplation? Even if it were possible to do so (which I don't believe it is, since the very spiritual practices and way of life of Thich Nhat Hanh are *inseparable from* the beliefs he is trying to live out), this religious system has no place for a personal God who has revealed Himself and whose revelation of Himself requires a response. Notably, neither the personal, identifiable God of the Bible, nor Jesus, are either mentioned or, I believe it is safe to say, in view in any way in such a discussion of the "kingdom of god" and the related peace he professes to derive from his particular form of spirituality.

All of the above "wisdom" presented through such "Super Soul Sundays" episodes may sound impressive and profound on the surface, but compared with the robust and complete revelation of God through the Bible, this amounts to no more than human wisdom which only demonstrates either a lack of the knowledge of, or a categorical denial of the written revelation of God in the Bible. This is the spiritual corollary of mass-produced junk food that has no nutritional value but tastes and looks good to the natural senses and human thinking. There is no discernible and consistent truth "signal" amidst this onslaught of spiritual "noise." Such proposed definitions of "God" as presented on her shows will ultimately be totally dissatisfying to anyone who is diligently and sincerely seeking the true knowledge of God. If anything, I would expect people only to be more confused after hearing such opinions about who "God" is. For Oprah, she revealed the bottom line spiritually for herself this way: "I have church within myself: I have church walking down the street. I believe in the God force that lives inside all of us, and once you tap into that, you can do anything." (Wikipedia, referencing Lowe, Janet, January 22, 2001. *Oprah Winfrey Speaks: Insights from the World's Most Influential Voice.* John Wiley &

Sons, p. 122). How can anyone come to a specific or saving knowledge of the one true God who has revealed himself through history and the written revelation of the Bible from someone who approaches "god" this way? About one key point here there can be no doubt or debate: the "god" she is referring to has nothing to do with the God revealed in the Bible but is an abstraction, an impersonal "force" whose sole purpose for her seems to be making all your dreams come true—like the genie of Aladdin's lamp, though an even more nameless one.

It needs to be pointed out before we wrap up this discussion that if there is any consistent theme or message coming through the theological and spiritual perspectives promoted by Oprah through her media platform, it would in fact be a strong "Oneist" flavor and thrust, as per Dr. Peter Jones' important insight presented in Chapter 4. In sync with the spreading popularity of such "Oneist" practices as yoga (Hinduism lite), and mindfulness (Buddhism lite), Oprah is helping usher a thoroughly pagan, anti-Christian spirituality (cloaked, ironically, in "Christian" window dressing) into our culture, and it seems to be working.

To be clear, if the one true God of the universe has gone to the extreme lengths to provide such a fully adequate written revelation of himself to the world as he has in the Bible, such definitions as presented above reveal either a complete lack of knowledge of scripture, or a denial and rejection of it. Of course knowing what the Bible says isn't enough—it also requires faith to not only accept but even to properly understand it. The "top spiritual thinkers" featured in this particular show demonstrate the utter failure of human minds, no matter how intelligent or how devoted to pursuing "truth," to know God correctly without direct divine revelation provided by God to us. The Bible makes it perfectly clear that God is on an altogether different level from man, and that no matter how spiritual, religious, or close to God we may think we are, as human beings we can never really approach godhood or divinity, as this verse clearly states (among many others): *For my thoughts are not your thoughts, neither are your ways my ways, declares the Lord. For as the heavens are higher than the earth, so are my ways higher than your ways and my thoughts than your thoughts.* (Isaiah 55:8-9) The question then becomes, when God has revealed himself in a such a robust and sufficient way, what would explain anyone, especially people at the level of intelligence of these, not to avail themselves of it, or to actually reject it?

Interestingly, Oprah's spirituality, and her massive impact on the spiritual climate of the larger culture, is powerfully and unflatteringly stated by a non-Christian and in fact "progressive" online magazine, *Slate*, in the following passage:

Perhaps more than any other single American, she is responsible for giving national platforms and legitimacy to all sorts of magical thinking, from pseudoscientific to purely mystical, fantasies about extraterrestrials, paranormal experience, satanic cults, and more . Most of the best-known prophets and denominational leaders in the New Age realm owe their careers to Winfrey. Her man Eckhart Tolle, for instance, whose books The Power of Now *and* A New Earth *sold millions of copies apiece, is a successful crusader against reason itself. "Thinking has become a disease," he writes, to be supplanted by feeling "the inner energy field of your body." The two of them conducted a series of web-based video seminars in 2008. New Age, because it's so American, so utterly democratic and decentralized, has multiple sacred texts. One of the most widely read and influential is Rhonda Byrne's* The Secret, *emphatically placed in the canon by Winfrey as soon as it was published a decade ago. "I've been talking about this for years on my show," Winfrey said during one of the author's multiple appearances on Oprah. "I just never called it* The Secret." The Secret *takes the American fundamentals, individualism and supernaturalism and belief in belief, and strips away the middlemen and most of the pious packaging—God, Jesus, virtue, hard work rewarded, perfect bliss only in the afterlife. What's left is a "law of attraction," and if you just crave anything hard enough, it will become yours. Belief is all. The Secret's extreme version of magical thinking goes far beyond its predecessors'. It is staggering. A parody would be almost impossible. It was No. 1 on the Times's nonfiction list for three years and sold about 20 million copies.* (https://slate.com/health-and-science/2018/01/oprah-winfrey-helped-create-our-irrational-pseudoscientific-american-fantasyland.html)

How refreshing and gratifying it is to hear those words of sanity coming from an online magazine which might be expected to be more sympathetic to Winfrey, at least politically. This commentary recognizes the truly delusional nature of the thought process advocated by Byrne and her comrades with religious zeal. I am indebted to *Slate* for finding the words to adequately denounce such irresponsible and self-serving nonsense for what it is. The more serious point to take from all of this is that many people who profess to be Christians, even those who go to church, may fail to recognize the demonic, antichrist spirit behind such teachings. In fact, the success of the book noted in the last sentence of the above quote indicates both the staggering influence Oprah has over millions, and the willingness (or susceptibility) of millions to follow her lead in spiritual matters. So while there are still plenty of people who have not yielded their ability to think rationally to such influences, a sober assessment of the ability of a sustained propaganda campaign from one of the nation's largest media empires to infiltrate the minds and eventually hearts of large segments of the population should be deeply alarming. Just as was observed in Germany under Hitler's rule, if you tell a big enough lie loudly enough and long enough from a point of strong influence, eventually most people will capitulate. But an important aspect of being a rock is having the knowledge of truth, clarity of mind, and freedom in Christ to reject such lies for what they are and continue to trust, serve and worship only the one true God who has revealed himself to the world in the pages of scripture.

Biblical Truth Requires a Binary Response

As I have come to see it, and as the foregoing examples hopefully illustrate, the Bible presents a binary option at the most fundamental level, namely that either we receive God's word as the unique, direct, complete and sufficient revelation by God of himself, or we do not. As noted, many theologians and pastors or teachers who identify themselves as Christians may be knowledgeable about the Bible, while at the same time rejecting much of the perspective it presents on important subjects such as sexuality, marriage, genders, the sanctity of life, the exclusivity of salvation through Jesus, and even the miracles, the virgin birth and the bodily resurrection of Jesus. But if we reject such biblical truth, we make ourselves the judge of scripture—and by extension, *of God*. Does that make any sense? Furthermore, if our conception of God is any different than the one he himself revealed, then we have by definition constructed an idol. Even saying God is "beyond knowing" does a great disservice to God rather than honoring him as it pretends to do, because he has graciously and lovingly revealed himself to us in scripture with a high level of depth and detail.

The high level of specificity in the Bible reaches its zenith in both importance and clarity in its account of the events surrounding the life, death and resurrection of Jesus Christ. We have a more than sufficient collection of direct, eyewitness, written accounts of what he said and did, as well as a great deal of interpretive scripture to explain it all by the inspiration of the Holy Spirit. So for a person to say God is beyond knowing is simply an admission that they simply don't know him yet. I want to give Oprah the benefit of the doubt and assume her motives are on some level pure and that she sincerely believes she is really helping humanity through this effort to bring spiritual enlightenment to the masses, but if her paradigm of spiritual reality misses the mark, or worse, is in opposition to the truth, is she really doing anyone any favors? On the other hand, could it be that since genuine, biblical Christianity clearly does not sell well nor have wide appeal, while the material she broadcasts never acknowledges the reality of sin and our rebellion from God which requires radical change in us, "pop spirituality" is a far better business proposition? Considering the unimaginable wealth she has acquired through her media empire, the last possibility certainly seems highly plausible. And that approach will certainly not get us to the Rock we need to be grounded on if we are to have unshakeable stability, reliability, integrity, confidence and peace in any and all conditions.

A relevant biblical passage speaking to the worthlessness of all idols, whether visible or ideological, is the following:

Your name, O LORD, endures forever, your renown, O LORD, throughout all ages. For the LORD will vindicate his people and have compassion on his servants. The idols of the nations are silver and gold, the work of human hands. They have mouths, but do not speak; they have eyes, but do not see; they have ears, but do not hear, nor is there any breath in their mouths. Those who make them become like them, so do all who trust in them. (Psalms 135:13-18)

The above verses begin by affirming God's reign and rule over all through all ages with a permanence and durability that could only come from the one eternal God and a most precious promise to his people. The second part presents the uselessness and sheer folly of believing in any idol. Although this passage references items that are made from "silver and gold, the work of human hands," the idols of our day are more often ideological, or worldly and carnal in nature so they are not as obvious as such primitive idols, but they are every bit as false, seductive and dangerous to "worship" as any other idol, maybe even more so. It should be mentioned what the essence of worship really is at this point. To worship anything is to devote yourself to, align yourself with, submit your life to (at least to some degree), and have your overall direction in life influenced by anything other than God and his revealed truth. I also think of idolatry in modern times as a power which, at the very least, exerts a gravitational pull over your life, drawing you away from the path (or way of life) you were born for, the one that it would be God's will for us to follow, and in a different direction serving lesser "gods" – in other words, idols. Remember the frog in the water? The water of the environment we are swimming in is heating up, and in my opinion is now approaching a full boil. To the extent we passively allow our minds to be bathed in the toxic brew of aberrant spirituality which our culture steadily presents to us with massive technological amplification, we will find ourselves, in the words of the Psalm above, "becoming like them"—a hollow counterfeit of life and truth, with our humanity violated and our souls warped and damaged. Let's now turn to consider more clearly how we can be so grounded in truth and the larger reality that we will be increasingly become the "rocks" we need to be in such an environment.

Questions for reflection:

1. Can you identify other "counterfeit rocks" (false spiritual ideologies) you have come across?
2. Why do you think such ideologies are so popular and lucrative?
3. What results might we expect from embracing such erroneous ideologies (or idols in general)?
4. How can we consistently and effectively refute such versions of counterfeit truth?

Chapter 6
Be a Rock!

If human beings are inherently fickle, fallible, unstable and ultimately unreliable by nature, becoming the kind of rock we have been exploring will require a fundamental change in our very nature. This change is not only for the benefit of other people in our lives, as important as that it, but it is also very much for our own benefit. In fact, the benefits are so manifold and so great that it would take another book just to describe them.

What are the "rock"-like qualities in view here? There is of course no one official list of such qualities that everyone would agree on, but in ancient times, Plato and his disciple Aristotle put forth a set of four qualities in the 4th century B.C. broadly recognized by non-Christian philosophers as well as Christian theologians to have particular merit. This was initially presented to best encapsulate a natural version of morality but was later embraced as valid by Thomas Aquinas in the 13th century as the "Cardinal Virtues." These four qualities are: prudence (or wisdom), courage (or fortitude), temperance (or self-control), and justice (or fairness). While it may be debatable how complete or definitive this list of character traits is for the purposes of living the most virtuous life possible, this seems to be a good starting point when considering how we should live, and it is hard to deny their merit, whether within or outside the Christian faith. Another, probably more familiar, but certainly more specific, set of character traits or behaviors at the core of the Jewish and Christian faiths would be the 10 Commandments found in Exodus 20:3-17 and Deuteronomy 5:7-21. The abbreviated version of these (my paraphrase) would be: 1. Do not worship any other gods but the one true God who has revealed himself; 2. Do not worship any created thing. 3. Do not take the name of the Lord God in vain. 4. Remember the Sabbath day. 5. Honor your father and mother. 6. Do not murder. 7. Do not commit adultery. 8. Do not steal. 9. Do not bear false witness. 10. Do not covet (desire for yourself) anything that does not belong to you. No doubt many people agree with most of these commandments and generally try to follow them. However, if we examine ourselves and our track record honestly, who of us can say we have successfully done all of these, or even that we never violated most (or all) of them or will in the future? This may seem so daunting as to be hopeless—and in fact it is, on our own strength. There is a still higher standard in the New Covenant (actually the same standard but just with a new emphasis on the real intent of the law) as stated by Jesus in Matthew 5:27-28, where he says, "You have heard that it was said, 'You shall not commit adultery.' But I say to you that everyone who looks at a woman with lustful intent has already committed adultery with her in his heart." A sober examination of this standard would lead us to the conclusion that this is not *humanly* possible, and that is true. But fortunately, there is divine assistance and empowerment to do this which is readily available to us all, which will be discussed in more depth further on.

Most people have heard of the "Golden Rule" and many can even quote it. This is really a command rather than a suggestion and is derived from Matthew 22:39 which states, "You shall love your neighbor as yourself." This statement by Jesus Christ was made around

Be a Rock!

30 A.D., but the same command is also present in the Old Testament in Leviticus 19:17, which uses identical wording and was written about 1400 years earlier. We could consider this to be another good "rule" to apply to the question of our character and rock-like stability. For the purposes of this book, I would suggest the following description of rock-like qualities we need to live out our lives in a way that is ultimately most successful in the greater scheme of life, not only for us but even more importantly for our spouses, children, grandchildren, extended families, friends, neighbors, colleagues in the workplace, and anyone else on whom our actions have impact: *Having the capacity, willingness, and quality of character which enables us to consistently do what is right, honorable and most beneficial for all whose lives we impact while obeying and honoring God in everything.* The great question, and the one to which this book is addressed, is how do we actually go about becoming such "rocks" for the greatest benefit of ourselves and others?

The Only Rock-Solid Foundation Provides Peace

I hope I have been able to make the case up to this point that we human beings are so inherently unstable that to be a rock to others we need to be firmly attached to a much larger and more reliable Rock which will never fail in any circumstance or condition. Because of our instability and that of the world in which we live, deep, consistent internal peace is elusive. Our own efforts to achieve such peace through popular self-help methods such as yoga, meditation, mindfulness, drugs, or even empty religious rituals, will fall short, especially when it is most needed. Part of the solution to this issue is to know the true Rock and to seek refuge in the one truly safe "stronghold" or "fortress" of God. Scripture speaks to this reality in many places in both the Old and New Testaments. Some Old Testament verses speaking to this concept include the following:

Listen to me, you who pursue righteousness, you who seek the Lord: look to the rock from which you were hewn, and to the quarry from which you were dug. (Isaiah 51:1)

The stone that the builders rejected has become the cornerstone. This is the Lord's doing; it is marvelous in our eyes. (Psalm 118:22-23)

He said, "The Lord is my rock and my fortress and my deliverer, my God, my rock, in whom I take refuge, my shield, and the horn of my salvation, my stronghold and my refuge, my savior; you save me from violence. (2 Samuel 22:2-3)

We have this as a sure and steadfast anchor of the soul, a hope that enters into the inner place behind the curtain, where Jesus has gone as a forerunner on our behalf... Hebrews 6:19

The Lord is my rock and my fortress and my deliverer, my God, my rock, in whom I take refuge, my shield, and the horn of my salvation, my stronghold. (Psalm 18:2)

He drew me up from the pit of destruction, out of the miry bog, and set my feet upon a rock, making my steps secure. (Psalm 40:2)

He only is my rock and my salvation, my fortress; I shall not be shaken. (Psalm 62:6)

Be to me a rock of refuge, to which I may continually come; you have given the command to save me, for you are my rock and my fortress. (Psalm 71:3)

Note the consistent themes presented in these verses: God as a rock (a solid, unshakeable foundation for life), a fortress (for strength and safety), and a refuge (safe place of rest, respite and protection from storms and attacks). This is not a form of poetic license or wishful thinking but a very sober perspective on just how vital and total our need for God is as a foundation for life and a refuge from all peril.

Ultimately the culminating and unifying statement on this truth is found in the New Testament, in Matthew 7:24-27 as discussed above. I believe this verse brings together all the critical elements to provide a summary declaration of supreme importance to anyone who desires to be such a "rock" as this book attempts to put forth. These elements include a) the words of Jesus/the Bible, b) our own lives represented by the house in the parable, c) the adverse conditions of life which are inevitable and to varying degrees constant, represented by the rain, floods and wind in the parable, d) the rock on which the wise man built his house, namely the teachings of Jesus, which by direct extension are represented by the entire Bible, and e) the sand which represents human wisdom, "pop" spirituality as described in the previous chapter, and any doctrine speaking to key issues of truth which is at variance with the word of God.

You may be wondering if it is valid for me to interpret the statement of Matthew 7:24-27 as implying that "these words of mine" Jesus mentions in verses 24 and 26 are, by extension, the "words" of the entire Bible. I believe it is clear that this is the best interpretations based on the rest of scripture, which testifies that *all* scripture is directly inspired by the Holy Spirit (2 Tim 3:16). The Bible is also clear that Jesus never said or did anything which was not directed by God the Father, working in him through the Holy Spirit. Since both Jesus and scripture are faithful at every point to the Holy Spirit and neither error nor inconsistency is possible in the Holy Spirit, there is perfect agreement, harmony and unity between the God-man Jesus Christ, the word of God (the Bible) and the Holy Spirit, all of which is in direct and continuous union with the Father. So I believe it is not just plausible, but actually self-evident that when Jesus refers to "my words" in Matthew 7:24, this statement applies by extension to the entire written revelation of God.

Another verse which describes God as an "everlasting rock" and raises the related and important issue of deep and abiding inner peace which is a component of and necessary for developing and maintaining the rock-like quality of character we are seeking is Isaiah 26:3-4:

You keep him in perfect peace whose mind is stayed on you, because he trusts in you. Trust in the Lord forever, for the Lord God is an everlasting rock.

In this verse, the everlasting Rock is identified as the Lord God. Trusting in Him — and being firmly attached to Him — not only makes you solid as a rock yourself, it provides you with perfect peace, which imparts a level of mental and emotional stability enabling you to be a source of stability for yourself and for others. I have personally found this peace, which includes the cessation of internal turmoil, restlessness and anxiety, but also a deep calmness and durable equipoise, to be an extremely important stabilizing power. It is an important principle that is an integral part of my ability to function as the rock I need to be in every area of my life. This verse also points out that trusting in the Lord has an eternal quality to it, since God is eternal and transcends time and space, elevating your groundedness above temporal human circumstances. This stabilizing groundedness is based on the eternally unchanging character and resources of an infinitely powerful and benevolent God and is therefore not subject to changing conditions or degradation of any kind at any time. The peace described in this verse is a supernatural gift, not a result of behavior modification, external conditions, a "positive mental attitude," or any other change we can make via our own resources, as helpful as those factors might be; this kind of peace that provides a deeply unshakable stability and fidelity at the point of greatest testing is indeed supernatural, supplied by God for our benefit and for His glory. While in this life it is true that the peace we experience will not be a continuous, uninterrupted condition given our own sin nature and the corruption of the world, the greater truth is that God has an infinite capacity to supply such peace to his people through the completed and irrevocable work of Jesus Christ, in his death on the cross, his resurrection, his ascension, and the sending forth of the Holy Spirit without measure into the hearts and lives of his people.

I began this book by pointing out the rising chaos and discord in our culture, attempting to make the case that mental, emotional and especially spiritual peace is more elusive than it has ever been, yet no less important or desirable. I think it is safe to say that all people crave that kind of peace, whether consciously or not, yet in our natural condition do not know how to find it. I can truly sympathize with that perspective, having been there myself, not only before my conversion but even afterwards in many ways for a long and difficult season. I may not have sought peace through some of the methods increasingly practiced and promoted in our society such as meditation, mindfulness, yoga, drugs and so forth, but because I was not really building my "house" (life) on the Rock, I was flighty and resorting to human (or natural) and flawed approaches to finding that peace. Of course I failed to really find it until I fully surrendered to the reign and will of God in my life and the authority of his written revelation over me. God has revealed to us the source of that deep, abiding, and durable peace in his word and through the giving of new birth, the regeneration of the Holy Spirit, with the associated promise of eternal life. This is a promise which is clear and definitive in scripture and should give anyone who has received Christ such a deep and encompassing peace as is beyond description:

The Lord is at hand; do not be anxious about anything, but in everything by prayer and supplication with thanksgiving let your requests be made known to God. And the peace of God, which surpasses all understanding, will guard your hearts and your minds in Christ Jesus. (Philippians 4:5b-7)

Identity As a Key To Being a Rock

Another important requirement to becoming the "rock" which we want, and God wants, us to be for the benefit of others and ultimately ourselves is understanding our *identity in Christ* and actually learning to think and operate as though that is our primary and overriding identity, because it is—for those who truly belong to him. Of course we do have other, lesser identities, related to such aspects of our identity as our family name and family history, our academic or other credentials, our professional role/status, our marriages, our children and their accomplishments, our socioeconomic status, our other affiliations and attachments such as churches, clubs or social causes. As important as all of these may be, none should be regarded as anywhere close to or in competition with our primary identity in Christ, which for the committed Christian becomes the one categorical, all-inclusive and comprehensive identity which defines us. This identity should be the starting point and frame of reference for who we understand ourselves to be, what our purpose is, and how we should then live out our lives. Resolving this is a necessary step toward true rock-like stability, reliability, integrity, character and all the key qualities we so desperately need to live effectively and in a way that is pleasing to God. Scripture has much to say on this subject of our identity in Christ. Jesus explicitly addressees this important point at the Last Supper in a number of ways, but a few relevant verses are the following:

"Holy Father, keep them in your name, which you have given me, that they may be one, even as we are one. While I was with them, I kept them in your name, which you have given me." (John 17:11b-12a)

This verse specifically refers to the followers of Christ as being "in your name, which you have given me," which I believe is a reference to the name of Jesus Christ, which is clearly identified as the name by which God's people are identified, as referenced in this verse:

Therefore God has highly exalted him and bestowed on him the name that is above every name, so that at the name of Jesus every knee should bow, in heaven and on earth and under the earth, and every tongue confess that Jesus Christ is Lord, to the glory of God the Father. (Philippians 2:9-11) The term "Christian" is the specific "name" or "identity" by which those who follow Christ, in other words, God's people, are identified. This term was first used in Antioch in the first century A.D. (referenced in Acts 11:26) and while it may originally have been used derisively by non-believers, it was embraced by the early church, much as persecution was accepted and expected, and the term's permanence and universal prevalence would seem to support its use as the best identifying term for God's people. Note that implied in this very term is the recognition that our allegiance as Christians is to the Lord Jesus Christ, not even to any particular church denomination or institution, and that should this allegiance require a change of religious or denominational affiliations, or for that matter key relationships in our lives, we must obey and be faithful to our Lord above all. Since the beginning, millions of people around the world have regarded their identity in Christ to be more precious than life itself, paying the ultimate price for it at the hands of their persecutors—and this is happening more now than at any previous time in history. This Christian identity must be so pre-eminent in our mindset and worldview that any other "identity" factor which undermines or opposes our primary identity in Christ will need to be dealt with, either removed completely from our lives, or at least decisively neutralized and negated. When it comes to our identity in Christ, we need a "faith firewall" which will identify and eliminate any competing identities or loyalties so that our primary one will not be compromised.

Another verse which speaks powerfully, even poetically, to our unique and privileged identity in Christ: *But you are a chosen race, a royal priesthood, a holy nation, a people for his own possession, that you may proclaim the excellencies of him who called you out of darkness into his marvelous light. Once you were not a people, but now you are God's people; once you had not received mercy, but now you have received mercy.* (1 Peter 2:9-10) While the point of this scripture is *not* to make us believe we are "better" than others, it does strongly convey the truth that in Christ we have a special and sacred status, so to speak, which should be cherished, valued, safeguarded, nurtured, honored, and recognized for its significance and distinctiveness. From that perspective we are to step out and "proclaim the excellencies of him who called you out of darkness and into his marvelous light." What higher or greater purpose than that could we have for living?

Eternal Life, Fruits of the Holy Spirit

Beyond this, our identity in Christ as sons and daughters of God gives us assurance of eternal life which can not be taken away by any human being, devil, angel, or any other power in the universe: *And this is the testimony, that God gave us eternal life, and this life is in his Son. Whoever has the Son has life; whoever does not have the Son does not have life.* (1 John 5:11-12). Please do not miss this point! God in his extravagant love and generosity offers all people eternal life, but the means by which God has appointed for this to occur is through his Son. Whether it seems fair or logical to our human minds, God in his infinite wisdom and goodness, "has qualified you to share in the inheritance of the saints in light. He has delivered us from the domain of darkness and transferred us to the kingdom of his beloved Son, in whom we have redemption, the forgiveness of sins." (Colossians 1:12-14)

Another, more familiar, verse that summarizes key theology with regard to this point is John 3:16-19: *For God so loved the world, that he gave his only Son, that whoever believes in him should not perish but have eternal life. For God did not send his Son into the world to condemn the world, but in order that the world might be saved through him. Whoever believes in him is not condemned, but whoever does not believe is condemned already, because he has not believed in the name of the only Son of God. And this is the judgment: the light has come into the world, and people loved darkness rather than the light because their works were evil.*

Ultimately, everything that is needed — including most importantly regenerative belief itself and the faith that enables us to perceive spiritual truths and the reality and influence of God in our lives and the world, to recognize our condition as it actually is in the sight of God, and which motivates us to surrender our wills to God, trusting Him — is all supplied by Him. When we consider that we are created beings which He created, and He is an uncreated eternal Spirit Who has the creative capacity and power to bring the universe with all the glorious creation we have come to know, it should be easy to recognize that everything was originated, created and animated by God. The Bible is the definitive sacred collection of writings which no human being — other than the handful of writers of the books contained in it, and even they were really just recipients of divine revelation — in any way contributed to, and hence we can only receive it with profound gratitude and awe. Consequently, our ability to take on the kind of nature and character that makes it possible for us to be a rock of reliability, integrity, grace, mercy, love, forgiveness, kindness, generosity, honesty is entirely derived from God through His word, His Holy Spirit, and the supernatural and common grace He so abundantly supplies to us at all times.

Another important verse, this one from the New Testament speaks to this truth: *But the fruit of the Spirit is love, joy, peace, patience, kindness, goodness, faithfulness, gentleness, self-control; against such things there is no law.* (Galatians 5:22-23)

Those in whom the Holy Spirit is pleased to dwell will, without exception (though imperfectly) when yielded to God's sovereign will over their lives, experience all of these fruits of the Holy Spirit, to a degree that will be apparent not only to the individual in question, but also to those who are close to him or her. Trusting in God as advocated in Isaiah 26:3, results in a level of peace, which implies a deep level of stability and reliability, and is the main prerequisite for being a rock for yourself or for others. The alternative – a state of confusion, doubt and anxiety – deprives us of the inner stability and peace we need to be a reliable rock for others. In addition to peace, consider the other fruits of the Holy Spirit listed above. In particular, consider faithfulness, patience, kindness, goodness and self-control. These would be the characteristics we would desire more than any other in a person on whom we depend such as a parent or a spouse, so if we wish to be as reliable and effective for good in the lives of those we care most about, wouldn't it be our top priority to pursue the acquisition of these fruits or gifts? There is only one way to accomplish this, which is to enter into this trust relationship with the Lord God Almighty. This is not a trifling matter. We can't fool God. He knows our hearts, far better than we do, and nothing is hidden from His view. As Hebrews 10:31 says, *It is a fearful thing to fall into the hands of the living God.* Yet it is also the most wonderful, freeing, joyful, empowering possible development that can happen in our lives.

Trusting in God, given such qualities and given the earlier observation of how unreliable all natural and man-made resources ultimately are, is the most rational, practical and wise thing we could possibly do. Yet it is so difficult for us. Why is that? I believe (and the Bible teaches) that our fallen, sinful nature causes us all to live in a state of rebellion from God by default. So to gain access to the benefits that God offers those who have been reconciled to Him, a great transaction needs to occur in which our sin and rebellion are forgiven by God and the righteousness of Jesus Christ, the only sinless man ever to live in perfect, sacrificial obedience, is credited to us in the sight of God. Once this occurs, we have unrestricted access to God through Jesus Christ and can begin the process of attaching (or, more accurately, being attached by the grace of God and the action of the Holy Spirit on us) firmly and eternally to this Rock.

1 Samuel 2:2 states, *There is none holy like the Lord: for there is none besides you; there is no rock like our God.* This verse emphasizes the uniqueness and exclusivity of the Lord's holiness, as well as His ability to serve as the one and only Rock that is 100% reliable at all times and provides a sure foundation and continuous stability under all conditions. If you have your doubts about this claim, remember we are talking about the God of the universe, not anything or anyone in the natural realm, but the same God who created the entire universe in all its stunning beauty, complexity, intricacy and scale. He does not change like human beings do. Some verses that speak to this truth are the following:

I am the Lord, and there is no other, besides me there is no God; I equip you, though you do not know me, that people may know, from the rising of the sun and from the west, that there is none besides me; I am the Lord, and there is no other. (Isaiah 45:5-6)

And:

Jesus Christ is the same yesterday and today and forever. (Hebrews 13:8)

These two verses speak strongly to the permanence and singularity of God's nature, character, utter uniqueness, authority and eternality, and such truth should provide strong encouragement that God does not change, that He reigns eternally over all, and that He is, or at least wants to be, directly involved in our lives on a very personal level. He provides us with the faith we need to recognize this truth and to know that we can count on it now and always.

The Ultimate Safe Space

While the recent phenomenon of "safe spaces" may strike many of us as rather odd, it is only one more example of the deep need people recognize at difficult times for a place of refuge where one can feel safe and secure. In addition to the perspective presented in this book that we humans, being fallible and fickle, need a solid and reliable foundation on which to base our very lives, God, being as merciful and loving as he is, also knows our great weakness, frailty and vulnerability, hence he is also presented repeatedly as our *refuge* in Scripture in a manner very similar to the way he is often presented as a rock. The point is that people have a deep need for a place of refuge from the storms of life, but the only reliable "safe space" or refuge is in fact the Lord God. The many ways we try in our natural state to seek refuge from the ongoing and sometimes unbearable stresses of life, whether it be alcohol, drugs, pornography, college "safe spaces" or otherwise, all have real drawbacks (and potential harm) and in any event fail to meet the deeper need for a place of refuge that is always reliable while making us more human rather than less so. The truth on this subject revealed by scripture is rather amazing: not only that God provides a place of refuge for us— he *is* that refuge for us, and much, much more. The beautiful poetic imagery of the Psalms such as "under the shadow of your wings I will take refuge" speaks to this important and universal need that human beings have for a "place" that they can go to feel safe. Although there are some saf*er* places in this world such as underground bomb shelters, there is no place of ultimate safety apart from God, because safety is in the end a *spiritual* matter. The only real safety is found in the Lord. But we can only approach him and find refuge in him on *his* terms, which is to recognize God's sovereignty, acknowledge and repent of our sin, receive forgiveness in Christ, and surrender our will to the will of God and seek his face continuously in his word, in prayer, in worship and in fellowship. Some good examples of Bible verses speaking to this need are the following:

God is our refuge and strength, a very present help in trouble. Therefore we will not fear though the earth gives way, though the mountains be moved into the heart of the sea, though its waters roar and foam, though the mountains tremble at its swelling. (Psalm 46:1-3)

Lead me to the rock that is higher than I, for you have been my refuge, a strong tower against the enemy. (Psalm 61:2b-3)

He who dwells in the shelter of the Most High will abide in the shadow of The Almighty. I will say to the Lord: "My refuge and my fortress, my God, in whom I trust." (Psalm 91:1-2)

Psalm 31 also begins with a similar focus on God as our place of refuge: *In you, O LORD, do I take refuge; let me never be put to shame; in your righteousness deliver me! Incline your ear to me; rescue me speedily! Be a rock of refuge for me, a strong fortress to save me! For you are my rock and my fortress; and for your name's sake you lead me and guide me; you take me out of the net they have hidden for me, for you are my refuge.* (Verses 1-3)

The New Testament and the gospel of salvation through Jesus Christ takes this concept of refuge even further with such passages as the following:

"Come to me, all who labor and are heavy laden, and I will give you rest. Take my yoke upon you, and learn from me, for I am gentle and lowly in heart, and you will find rest for your souls. For my yoke is easy, and my burden is light." (Matthew 11:28-30)

This is for myself and so many, one of the most comforting and peace-inducing verses in all the Bible. It is a remarkable statement that the incarnate Lord makes, in which he (and by extension God the Father) not only becomes directly accessible, but offers to exchange our intolerable burdens which we are unable to bear for his light burden which we can easily bear by his grace. Despite being the Creator and ruler of the universe, he stoops all the way down to our earth-bound and broken levels to offer his comfort, security and power. Only God could do this for us.

"O Jerusalem, Jerusalem, the city that kills the prophets and stones those who are sent to it! How often would I have gathered your children together as a hen gathers her brood under her wings, and you were not willing!" (Matthew 23:37)

This is another startlingly tenderhearted and loving statement for a recalcitrant people, one which moved Jesus to tears as he spoke it. The image of God as a mother hen gathering her chicks under her wings to protect them with her very life strongly reveals the level of love he has for his people, seemingly despite their persistent rebellion.

"Let not your hearts be troubled. Believe in God; believe also in me. In my Father's house are many rooms. If it were not so, would I have told you that I go to prepare a place for you? And if I go and prepare a place for you, I will come again and will take you to myself, that where I am you may be also." (John 14:1-3)

Although Jesus makes this statement to his disciples at the Last Supper, by extension this promise applies to all faithful followers of Jesus. How extraordinarily personal and loving such a truth and statement is, yet such promises are true and have power to sustain all his faithful through the most difficult of circumstances.

"I have said these things to you, that in me you may have peace. In the world you will have tribulation. But take heart; I have overcome the world." (John 16:33)

This is one of the great summary statements of the ultimate and complete victory of Jesus Christ over all that opposes the reign and rule of God, including our sin nature, the spectre of our own deaths, and the devil with his entire kingdom of fallen angels (demons). This is a promise and a truth to lay hold of firmly.

And the peace of God, which surpasses all understanding, will guard your hearts and your minds in Christ Jesus. (Philippians 4:7)

This could be thought of as a companion verse to the prior one (John 16:33) as the knowledge of Jesus' victory over the world results in "the peace of God which surpasses all understanding." And this is a most precious truth to those of us who know it experientially.

There are many other clear descriptions of God as the refuge and the only one that provides ultimate safety from any and all danger for His people. This is not to say that God's people are always physically safe, but it is to declare with total confidence that our souls and our spirits, what makes us who we are and the essence of our selves, which has an eternal future, is safe in a way no other conditions or person could ever make us. The promises of security constantly offered by the world, including financial or physical security, all have limits—as well as an expiration date! When we are facing death, any earthly security, whether wealth, power, physical safety and security, or anything else we might count on to protect or validate us in this life, becomes completely useless. Even our closest family and friends (should be be blessed with them) while able to comfort us to some degree, can not provide us with the depth of grace, confidence or peace we need in the hour of our deaths—much less all such other material and earthly resources. In stark contrast, it is *particularly at* such critical moments of testing or ultimately of death when we can really appreciate the true value of the complete and totally reliable security we have in God, and in Him alone.

Redeemed and Rescued from God's Wrath

On an even more serious note pertaining to death, the Bible presents a clear though difficult reality of a judgment to come after we die. Sin and rebellion against a good, just and holy God *necessarily* results in his wrath, and ultimately his judgment on people. The greatest threat to us is actually not even in this earthly life, but in the final judgment, and all of our greatest and most impressive human efforts to avert this reality is futile. There is only one possible refuge for us against this most ominous eventuality: God Himself. This may seem ironic, but I believe if you think it through it will make good sense. For God to declare us innocent, to forgive us completely, and then to take it a giant step further by attributing the righteousness of Christ to our own personal "accounts" with God, is only something God has the prerogative or authority to do. We ourselves have no ability or recourse on a human level to address this greatest of all human problems. But in keeping with his nature which is infinitely good, loving and forgiving, while also not violating his holiness and righteousness, he sent his son into the world to redeem humanity—but at the highest possible price of his own life, even taking on himself (Jesus) the curse and the cumulative sin of the entire human race (conditionally) while he hung on the cross in the worst possible physical and mental agony for about 6 hours until he died. His last words on the cross were, "It is finished!" What was finished at the moment of his sacrificial death? The open offer to all humanity of forgiveness of sins and restoration to a relationship with God as a result of repentance and placing our faith and trust in Christ alone. When he rose from the dead on the third day after his death, he confirmed his identity as the Son of God and birthed the church, which is his body of true and committed believers in the world, a reality which transcends all denominational, cultural, geographical, language, age, gender or racial differences or barriers, so definitive, universal and supernatural a reality it is. Those who put their full trust in Jesus Christ have the reward already in this life of such extended fellowship in the global communion of the saints which he and only he made possible by his death and resurrection followed by the outpouring of the Holy Spirit on his people. Applying this set of truths and the underlying reality to our lives will provide us with the ultimate "refuge" which is God himself as well as his people on this earth and his written word.

You may still be wondering what is so allegedly special or unique about the God of the Bible. What about all the other faith traditions or spiritual practices and belief systems? Can't they also provide a firm foundation under the most difficult and extreme conditions?

From its beginning to its end, the Bible presents one overarching, unified story of the redemption of humanity which simply has no rival or parallel in any other faith or belief set. No other writings or set of writings so honestly reveals the sin condition of all people like the Bible does, reveals a loving God who loves us even while we were in active rebellion (sin) against His sovereign rule, provides the definitive solution to this predicament of our failure to meet the requirements of God, and then provides assurance, even the certainty, of our accepted, forgiven condition before Him and our destiny to enjoy eternal life with Him in heaven. Speaking for myself, I can genuinely say that were it not for the supernatural revelation of Jesus Christ to me and the new life he gave me when I was 24 years old, I realize now that I would not have been able to come to these conclusions or be motivated to share these thoughts. I recognize that because of our sinful condition, without such supernatural help from God, we are not able on our own to perceive the world, ourselves, or reality as they really are. Nor will we be able to discern good and evil, or have true wisdom in prioritizing our lives and living productive and faithful lives that are pleasing to a holy God without the revelation of truth to us by God.

A different type of illustration of the principle of the enduring permanence and stabilizing truth quality of the scriptures is that even the chosen people of God before the Messiah's arrival (the ancient Jews) failed repeatedly and often dramatically at their assignment, given them by God, of remaining faithful to God and avoiding idolatry in its many forms. The Old Testament, throughout both the historical and prophetic writings, is unsparingly and extensively clear about the rampant prevalence of this problem in ancient Israel and is one of the most important themes of the entire Old Testament. Despite this, perhaps the greatest purpose for which God chose a specific group of people to interact with, quite dramatically, over several thousand years, was to accurately record and meticulously preserve the writings that chronicle their history of interaction with God, as well as much wisdom literature and prophetic revelations. Despite the almost universal theme of apostasy and idolatry on the part of the Israelites throughout the Old Testament, one thing they did do amazingly well was carefully document, collect, select and then preserve for millennia the sacred writings, as directed by God to do so. They understood that they were doing this for future generations and in preparation for the coming of the anointed One, the Messiah of God. Because of their faithfulness to this assignment of God (which no doubt He helped them with supernaturally throughout the many centuries when the sacred writings were composed and collected) and thanks to the printing and publishing technology which later became available to increasingly large percentages of the world's population, much of the human population has access to the Bible in their own languages and so can evaluate the merits of these writings themselves. What we see is that the word of God endures and remains faithful throughout the generations despite the periodic unfaithfulness of His chosen people and the arrival and departure of many world empires as well as ideologies and religions.

Fortunately, if we humble ourselves just enough to ask God to show us if these things are true, to make Himself known to us, to "turn on the lights" of our spiritual understanding, He will do so. The most important step in beginning a life that allows you or me to be a rock to other people and under any conditions is to come to a saving knowledge of God through Jesus Christ. After that bridge has been crossed, then our privilege and our responsibility is to continually press into a deeper, more vital and more accurate knowledge of God. Importantly we should note that since God is a living Person, this knowledge is more analogous to "knowing" another person well. God is not an inert "subject" to learn, much less master, but He is knowable to the degree it is possible to "know" an infinite, eternal, omnipotent, omnipresent and omniscient God. He has gone to great lengths, often at the cost of the shedding of much blood of His people, to reveal Himself to us perfectly and definitively and comprehensively enough for all our purposes and needs in this regard, which He did in the Bible.

If you have never done this before, I invite you to simply ask God to reveal Himself to you. You might pray like this: *Lord God, I want to know if you are for real. I recognize my inability to do this without your help. Please show me you are real, and if the Bible is your written revelation of yourself, please show me that as well. I acknowledge my need for your help even to do that. I thank you for listening to me and will do all that I can to accept and honor what you reveal of yourself to me. Thank you. In Jesus' name.*

When God reveals Himself to people, He usually does so inwardly, by imparting a supernatural spiritual knowledge of Him within you. Very few people have ever had a vision of God the Father, though many have had visions and dreams of Jesus Christ, a phenomenon that appears to be increasing in the current era. There are dramatic and undeniable accounts of people who did not believe in Him having a vision of Him even with Him speaking to them very specifically in answer to their prayer. God can do anything He wants and will reveal Himself to you in a way that He pleases. I have come to believe that God will do that which is not only for our greatest possible good but also that which glorifies Him most, so often how He does this is not how, or in the timeframe, we would like or hope. Nevertheless, He does answer all sincere, humble prayers in His time and in His way.

If God has been gracious to you and revealed enough of Himself to bring you to a knowledge of your sin and your need for forgiveness and salvation, and if you have not yet done so, to be forgiven and restored to a right relationship with God in which you become adopted into His family and become an heir to all the promises and rights and privileges of the family of God, you need to: a) recognize your sin and need for forgiveness; b) repent, asking for God to forgive you; c) commit your life to Jesus Christ, acknowledging Him as King of kings and Lord of lords (Matt. 28:18); and d) receive Him into your heart, being reborn spiritually (John 3:3). If you did this with a sincere heart, begin thanking God for His infinite forgiveness and goodness toward you, for providing His Son to die on a cross for your sins, and praise Him for his surpassing greatness and lovingkindness to all people, as supremely revealed in Jesus. Then devote yourself to growing in the knowledge of and obedience to Him, seeking every opportunity to read and study scripture, worship, pray, fellowship, and serve God. Find a faithful, inviting, Bible-believing, Spirit-filled church and engage deeply with that local body of believers. Be open to His vision for your life and be willing to surrender yours to Him. Recognize He will change the way you view the world and yourself, but that change is from an inaccurate and inadequate vision to an accurate and entirely adequate one.

Key Disciplines for Spiritual Growth

Some of the most valuable practical disciplines I can suggest to assist you to grow in your faith and rock-solid connection to God include the following:

- Bible study: there are no shortcuts to a deep and intimate knowledge of God and developing a Kingdom (of God) perspective on life—it requires regular diet of Bible reading and study. Most Bible translations can be used for this purpose, but I would highly recommend a version in your native language that is contemporary but faithful to the original texts. In my opinion, the best of these is the English Standard Version (ESV) as it combines all of these qualities unusually well, and the ESV Study Bible by Crossway is a truly outstanding study Bible with many notes, articles, scholarly (but easily understandable) introductions to each book of the Bible, many maps and the best illustrations I have seen in any Bible to bring the material alive and help you understand it. There are many reading plans which can easily be found online and downloaded to make it possible to get through the entire Bible in 1 year. There are also Bibles in which the books of scripture have been rearranged and bound into a book where the readings are by date and may include readings from the Old Testament, New Testament, Psalm and Proverbs in manageable chunks that can be easily read each day. The most important thing is to make it a regular part of your daily life and to feed deeply on God's word as something God is using to personally communicate with you.

- Prayer: This is arguably the one discipline and practice which most separates serious followers of Christ from the more casual or less committed. Prayer is the lifeblood of the Christian along with the Bible. Sincere, regular, fervent prayer is a necessary practice for anyone who seeks to know God's will and have the insight, wisdom, courage and power to carry it out. It is a most sacred activity which when done properly and from a humble and deeply reverential place can and should actually bring us into the very presence of God, even into his throne room in the spirit realm. God in inherently relational and personal and it is clear in scripture that his will is for all his followers to have an intimate and ongoing personal relationship with him which they actively nurture and intentionally cultivate, much as you would with your spouse or best friend. There is no substitute for this, and doing so has a profound impact on our hearts and minds, transforming us into the men and women of God which we were created and intended by God to be. The Apostle Paul's exhortation, "Do not be conformed to this world, but *be transformed* by the renewal of your mind, that by testing you may discern what is the will of God, what is good and acceptable and perfect." (Romans 12:2, emphasis added) The transformation which Paul writes about by the inspiration of the Holy Spirit requires a steady diet of scripture *and prayer*, at least daily but if possible multiple times throughout the day (the ultimate goal being to learn how to "pray without ceasing" as 1 Thessalonians 5:17 instructs us). Prayer ultimately must become a way of life or the flesh/the world/the devil will not have much difficulty eventually rendering us ineffective for anything good and significant in God's eyes.

- Fellowship: As pointed out in the previous section, God is a deeply relational by nature; we see this in the very reality of the Trinity, but we can also observe that God made people as social, or relational, beings. This is obviously true in every sphere of life, but this truth has particular significance within the context of the body of believers, or in other words the true church. There is a supernatural synergy that occurs when several (or more) people are gathered in the name of Jesus and yielded to his Lordship, and this is an important mechanism in the way the Lord does the mysterious but essential work of honing and refining us into the kinds of people he wants us to be. It is also a source of great joy and blessing for the participants and provides a kind of divine refreshment and encouragement that we all need in undertaking the difficult assignment of surrendering our wills to God and following Jesus. In addition, as I have experienced extensively and as scripture states, there is an "iron sharpens iron" (see Proverbs 27:17) effect of close longitudinal relationships within the context of fellowship in Christ which is one of the major functions of the (true) church or body of Christ in the world.

- <u>Worship</u>: I believe this is a poorly understood and greatly underappreciated aspect of a complete and effective life in relationship with God—and I certainly have made the mistake of taking it for granted. It would be difficult, perhaps impossible, to overstate the transformative and relational effects of genuine worship "in Spirit and in truth" (John 4:23) In fact, it should be evident that the highest activity and ultimate purpose for which we were created and born is actually to worship the true and living God in this way. Doing so is transformative as the Holy Spirit works through us to enable us to worship God out of loving, thankful, reverential awe, for his glory, honor and praise. When it is genuine and not a mechanical, rote and repetitive activity, there is nothing better that we can experience, or purpose we can fulfill, in this life. It has been pointed out (as masterfully done in <u>Addictions: A Banquet In The Grave—Finding Hope in the Power of the Gospel</u> by Edward T. Welch, for example) that all addiction is, in essence, a "worship disorder," and the best and most effective cure to any and all addictions is right worship "in spirit and in truth."

- <u>Memorizing Scripture</u>: I think of this as a process of engraving scripture on the 'hard drive' of your heart and mind, where it can reside permanently and is immediately available at any time it is needed. This is a labor of love for scripture and for

God, recognizing that there are multiple levels of benefit and blessing in doing so, one of which I believe is to make your mind sharper and your memory stronger, not for the purpose of making more money or impressing more people, but for the purpose of serving and glorifying God more effectively. I have memorized verbatim many sections of scripture in the old and new testaments, but some of my favorite passages are a number of the psalms I have memorized, and I would particularly commend to memorization Psalms 1, 16, 19, 23, and 103 which are ones I have memorized and I believe are especially good and beneficial. These psalms have also become only more precious to me over time, and the deep spiritual blessing they provide whenever I recite and meditate on them can not be adequately expressed in words.

• Memorizing hymns and worship songs: Committing the words (all of them) of some of the best hymns and more contemporary worship songs, and singing or reciting them to yourself (or even to others) regularly is a powerful and impactful spiritual exercise and is a great source of joy to the believer. This has been an important and essential feature of the shared life and connectedness of God's people from ancient times to the present. As we can see occurring very early in scripture (starting in Exodus chapter 15 with the "Song of Moses and Miriam" celebrating the safe passage of the people of Israel through the Red Sea on dry ground and the destruction of the pursuing army of Pharaoh as the water swept back over them), with all 150 of the Psalms being hymns for the Israelites, and this continues through the New Testament with many examples as well as this exhortation to the early church: *And do not get drunk with wine, for that is debauchery, but be filled with the Spirit, addressing one another in psalms and hymns and spiritual songs, singing and making melody to the Lord with your heart, giving thanks always and for everything to God the Father in the name of our Lord Jesus Christ, submitting to one another out of reverence for Christ.* (Ephesians 5:19). There are many great hymns and worship songs whose lyrics are well worth memorizing. One song which summarizes the gospel and its overwhelming benefits for the believer with unusual clarity and beauty is *In Christ Alone,* by Keith Getty and Stuart Townend (©2002), the first stanza of which follows:

In Christ alone my hope is found;
He is my light, my strength, my song;
This cornerstone, this solid ground,
Firm through the fiercest drought and storm.
What heights of love, what depths of peace,
When fears are stilled, when strivings cease!
My comforter, my all in all—
Here in the love of Christ I stand.

Just the first stanza above provides a clear presentation of the core truth upon which this book is based in that only Christ provides the foundation we need in all of life, but especially when the greatest difficulties arise. The accompanying music is also deeply beautiful and appropriately majestic in keeping with the content of the lyrics. I have memorized it (which is not difficult if you listen to the song enough—I recommend the version by Keith and Kristen Getty) and would recommend anyone to do the same, as it can serve as a valuable jewel in your devotional and spiritual armamentarium. Such a worship song is, in my opinion, saturated in the word of God and the Holy Spirit, which gives it real power to bring needed change to our souls, as well as to boost our faith and give us an abiding hope that no one can take away from us.

Another particularly good, though much older, hymn which summarizes key elements of the Christian faith while also emphasizing the central paradigm of God as our only firm foundation is My hope is built on nothing less by Edward Mote (c.1834), an except from which follows:

> *My hope is built on nothing less*
> *Than Jesus' blood and righteousness;*
> *I dare not trust the sweetest frame,*
> *But wholly lean on Jesus' name.*
> *On Christ, the solid Rock, I stand;*
> *All other ground is sinking sand...*
> *In every high and stormy gale,*
> *My anchor holds within the veil.*

In this hymn, the term "hope," as with the "house" in the parable of Matthew 7:24, implies a person's very life; likewise, "Jesus' blood and righteousness" cited in this hymn metaphorically represent the truth which is ultimately expressed in the words of Jesus mentioned in Matthew 7:24, which for us is the Bible, as well as the term "the gospel." Such hymns provide an easily memorized focus for contemplation of some of the greatest and most essential truths revealed to us by God while reminding us that we are still fallen, sinful human beings approaching an infinitely holy God and seeking His mercy, grace and help. Knowing the melody and being able to sing such worship songs to yourself or even perhaps to others embeds it in our memories and allows the glorious and freeing truths contained therein to penetrate our hearts deeply. This draws us closer to God, or to apply the rock metaphor, helps us become more firmly and deeply embedded into the Rock so that we may then in turn progressively become the rock we need to be to the other people in our lives. I encourage you to explore the realm of worship music and hymns, both contemporary and traditional, as both genres provide a stunning wealth of rich material for this very purpose. Also bear in mind that, while the melody and power of the music can be very uplifting and even inspiring, it is mainly the *words* that carry the spiritual power and impact for our benefit. So the key with hymns and worship music is the words, which like scripture can bring light and life to the believer. Of course, the scripture is always authoritative, while the content and quality of anything extra-scriptural, including worship music, needs to be examined in the light of Scripture and with the help of the Holy Spirit. Hymns such as the two above are, in my opinion, completely consistent with scripture and the gospel, not only in basic content but in the emphasis placed on key themes, and convey great power as they articulate truth that has the power to change lives and set us truly free. In addition, the music component can be inspired and anointed such that the hymn becomes even more powerfully uplifting than it would be based on the words alone and the words and the music become synergistic to God's glory and our profound, and even eternal, benefit. Thankfully, there are a large number of excellent traditional hymns such as Rock of Ages and more contemporary worship songs such as Christ Alone to suit your personal worship needs and preferences, as well as your musical tastes.

Additional Avenues for Spiritual Growth

Becoming a rock as discussed up to this point clearly is not just a matter of making a few changes in what we are doing or how we do it. This process touches every area of our life as it is a core matter of our character and mindset. Consequently, no activity, responsibility or concern of life is out of bounds or off-limits to the application of this paradigm. There are too many aspects of life to address them effectively in this regard, but I believe a few more are particularly worth pointing out. For the sake of simplicity, these will simply be listed in bullets below:

- Tithing, or giving 10% of your income to the church and effective para-church ministries;
- Fasting, which can take various forms, but involves voluntarily foregoing food and drink to varying degrees and for varying lengths of time to allow more focus on the spiritual and developing a reliance on the grace of God;
- Serving, whether in the church, on the missions field, or in local, national or international charities with a compatible mission, or in hospitality, or taking time to help a friend, neighbor or family member with something difficult or important;
- Identifying and eliminating bad habits and addictions (including socially acceptable ones) which requires the grace of God as you yield to God's will over every area of your life;
- Being generous and willing to share of our resources, including money, especially with those whose needs are greatest, recognizing that every good thing we have comes from the hand of God.

Another point to carefully consider is the importance of true holiness (not outward piety) for God's people. God is perfectly holy. He is Spirit and there is not the least shadow of corruption or imperfection in Him. He calls us all, but especially his people, to holiness. Nothing unholy will be allowed in heaven (how we, all being less than perfectly holy, can make it into heaven can only be explained by the righteousness of Jesus Christ imputed to us as a result of our faith in him, but to address this subject would require its own book). Holiness is not the same thing as outward perfection, but is a spiritual condition that is possible by God's grace and supernatural help, and has to do with the condition of our hearts and our obedience to His will in all areas of our lives to the best of our ability. Although difficult in one sense, we are called to make significant changes in the way we live and inevitably in some of our relationships, and to bring our thoughts, words and actions in alignment with His will as much as possible. We are to reflect His glory, but that will not happen unless we seriously and deliberately pursue holiness and take on the quality of holiness in how we live. Some verses which speak to this point are the following:

But as the one who called you is holy, you also are to be holy in all your conduct; for it is written, Be holy because I am holy. (1 Peter 1:15-16, CSB)

Therefore come out from among them and be separate, says the Lord… (2 Corinthians 6:17a, CSB)

Come out of her, my people, so that you will not share in her sins or receive any of her plagues (Revelation 18:4, CSB)… and "be holy as I am holy…"

As is the case in everything else having to do with our relationship with God, the call to holiness is a call to increasing levels of freedom, joy and life. This requires a deliberate and progressive disengagement from the fallen world system (the "her" in Revelation 18:4) which is, as scripture tells us, under the dominion of the devil — in other words, the spiritual energy that predominates in the world system, whether in the media or entertainment (music, movies, etc.) or higher education or the political and business realms, predominantly originates from and is sustained by the devil, from the perspective of scripture. Of course, God through His Holy Spirit is actively (though quietly for the most part) at work in this broken and fallen world, and He is also sovereign over everything the devil is trying to do. Still, due to the sin nature of humanity and the reality of a spiritual arch-adversary to God, the devil, the world system has a fallenness to it that leads to patterns of sin and bondage and blinds the eyes of people to the reality and glory and love and benevolent purposes of God toward us. To overcome this influence, while it needs to be individualized for our specific issues and circumstances, requires serious commitment to a life operating by faith and characterized by holiness. As has been stressed above, the Bible represents the primary resource to assist us in the great undertaking of becoming holy as he is holy, and consequently it is of the highest importance to not only know it by reading it regularly, but to so internalize it that it becomes our paradigm of reality — since it is the only accurate one presented in writing for all humanity and for all time.

Questions for reflection:

1. Have you personally surrendered your life over to God yet? If not, why not?

2. Is there any possession, relationship, affiliation (including to a church denomination) or credential you would not be willing to give up if it is hindering your relationship with Jesus Christ?

3. Can you identify any habit or substance you may reflexively turn to as a "refuge" from the stress or pressures of life, rather than turning to God alone (and his word) as that refuge?

4. Even if you believe you are not holding anything back from God's rule over your life, are there any practices or disciplines (such as discussed above) which you could cultivate in order to become more fully productive and effective as the rock God designed you to be?

Chapter 7
Being a Rock in Key Areas of Life

Every relationship, commitment and responsibility we are given in this life represents an opportunity to do good, which is to say to effectively serve and glorify God's good will for us and for humanity, or to fail to do so. There are a limited number of key areas in our lives in which living out this truth will result in exponential and lasting benefit to many, and in which failing to do so will have significant and far-reaching harmful effects to many, often including those for whom we most care about and are most responsible to. The following section considers several of the most important and representative of these in an effort to bring this insight further to life for you.

Being a Rock In Marriage

I suspect most people will agree with the perspective that marriage (as traditionally defined) represents the core foundation of human civilization that, more than any other single factor, is the key to human flourishing. I certainly am convinced of this truth after 32 years of marriage and raising four children. This perspective has always seemed to me to be a given, even long before discovering how the Bible deals with this subject. Unprecedented societal pressure to radically alter the definition, importance and role of marriage has the potential to undermine God's purposes for marriage for the benefit of all people and society, but we will not attempt to address this massive issue here. Rather, this section is intended for people who are married or plan to get married, particularly if children are or will be involved.

I have come to regard, as do many wise authors who have written on the subject, marriage as a kind of refining furnace in which we are formed by relentless heat and pressure into the person God wants us to become. The radical change of status from a single individual to a married person is difficult to overstate, and the spiritual implications are highly significant for the parties involved. It would probably be safe to say that a mixture of noble – or at least idealistic – and selfish motives are involved in every person's desire and decision to get married. What one begins to discover once married, often as soon as the honeymoon, if not soon thereafter, is that you have to make some big changes in the way you think, live and prioritize if you are going to have a successful and therefore happy marriage. Of course, part of the difficulty in marriage is not only dealing with our own self-centeredness, but we are permanently committed to another person who has the same difficult struggle. In addition to that, all people enter into marriage in a broken state, as a consequence of experiences, conditions and relationships in their lives prior to marriage, as well as their own poor past and ongoing decisions and habits, both mentally and bodily.

This may sound like a potentially hopeless scenario, and recognizing the truth of these observations certainly makes it easier to understand the extremely high divorce rate we see in the current era, not to mention the phenomenon of couples living together as though they were married even though they are not, with such couples increasingly having children in that context, while rarely in our current culture feeling as though they are out of step with the rest of society or doing anything wrong in the process. After all, the prevailing mentality reasons, the failure rate of marriage is high and many people come from broken homes to begin with, so "test-driving" a relationship, living together and even in many cases having children outside of marriage, seems to most people to be far more enlightened than problematic. This is a big subject in and of itself and I do not intend to tackle it, but I am just pointing out that the conditions within our society for marriage are inhospitable and becoming more unfavorable, it seems to me, quite rapidly. This context only compounds the difficulty of having a successful marriage considering the other, more personal, factors mentioned previously.

The key point of this book could not be more applicable to the subject of marriage, or put another way, marriage is arguably the most important example of a domain in which the application of the core insight of this book is most needed. But I do not present this perspective as though it were an academic subject matter, but only after living it out (imperfectly, of course) for many years in my own marriage. So if the word of God is the solid rock foundation for life, what does it actually say on the subject of marriage?

Many books have, of course, been written on the that very question, and the subject is very big, but here I will just share a few verses that I, and many other authors have found, to be particularly important for marriage. The first marriage-specific verse in the Bible that has huge implications for all marriages and for all time, is the following:

> *Therefore a man shall leave his father and mother and*
> *be joined to his wife, and they shall become one flesh.*
> (Genesis 2:24).

This verse indicates that when a man or a woman enters into marriage, the primary responsibility for, and accountability to, any other human being becomes to their spouse rather than to their parents as would have normally been the case up to the point of marriage. This statement clearly implies that the bond of marriage takes precedence over every other human relationship, and that the depth of that bond is nothing less than "becoming one flesh." This perspective begins to speak to the seriousness of the commitment involved. Marriage is the representative covenant relationship. The meaning of *a covenant* has been lost somewhat in our culture, but it represents the highest and most solemn form of promise or commitment which one party can make to another. The consequences of violating a covenant in the Old Testament were generally extreme and usually involved the loss of life of the offending party. While thankfully our culture does not support capital punishment for infidelity or divorce, the importance of this particular covenant relationship cannot be exaggerated, particularly in terms of its impact on the future generations that may result from it.

The next section of scripture is one that some would argue is most important of all on the subject of marriage:

> *Husbands, love your wives, as Christ loved the church and gave himself up for her, that he might sanctify her, having cleansed her by the washing of water with the word, so that he might present the church to himself in splendor, without spot or wrinkle or any such thing, that she might be holy and without blemish. In the same way husbands should love their wives as their own bodies. He who loves his wife loves himself.* (Ephesians 5:25-28) *Wives, submit to your own husbands, as to the Lord. For the husband is the head of the wife even as Christ is the head of the church, his body, and is himself its Savior. Now as the church submits to Christ, so also wives should submit in everything to their husbands.* (Ephesians 5:22-24) *However, let each one of you love*

> *his wife as himself, and let the wife see that she respects*
> *her husband.* (Ephesians 5:28)

So to summarize, given the importance of this passage, the roles and mindset required by the husband and wife are as follows: a) the husband leads as head of the marriage in sacrificial love, seeking to unconditionally love his wife, protect her and their children (if necessary at the risk of his own life), provide for all the material needs of his family (or at least make every effort to), and serve as the spiritual leader of the household under the ultimate Lordship of Jesus Christ; and b) the wife is to unconditionally respect her husband in view of his God-given assignment as described in the foregoing, with consistent, willing, and loving support of, and submission to, his leadership, both in spiritual and practical areas of their shared life, not because the man is better, smarter or preferred, but in joyful, willing obedience to God's good will and purposes for marriage, and by extension for the family.

As you may have noticed, the word of God is shockingly countercultural in the area of marriage. However I, and innumerable other people of goodwill (with the best intentions for both husband and wife and, by extension, their children), have concluded that it is in fact correct. Far more than correct, in fact, but rather the definitive truth and supernatural insight that is the key to understanding and succeeding in marriage. If God actually created men and women along with the rest of creation as the Bible clearly states, and if he is good and has good intentions for, and desires to bless us through us and for our marriages, and if the Bible is in fact reliably accurate with regard to the subjects on which it speaks, then anyone who is or will someday be married would be wise to pay close attention to scripture on this topic. And it is an amazing and beautiful thing that throughout all 66 books of sacred scripture, there is clarity, consistency, congruence and harmony in every place where the subject of marriage is addressed.

God designed men and women differently, and these differences are for good and noble purposes, with marriage and the family in view. When people work with rather than against their God-given design with their gender-determined characteristics in the context of marriage, great blessings and optimal productivity for good will result. Unfortunately, our understanding of these gender-based design differences is faulty, particularly as our culture has done away with the biblical perspective on this important area of life. As a result, I believe we need the revealed truth of the Bible to speak to this critical domain of life, or we will miss it – or at least abuse and misunderstand – completely.

The reason why the usual objections to the above verses from Ephesians are, in my opinion, misguided and misinformed, is that any such objections are based on an erroneous understanding of the differences between men and women, and the purposes for which marriage was instituted by God. The distinctive differences in the ways men and women were designed displays the manifold wisdom and indeed the glory of God. There are certain characteristics and qualities embedded into all men by design, and different ones embedded into all women by design. And these differences are complimentary, synergistic (especially in marriage), and reveal the wisdom and good purposes and intentions of God, to his glory. God's personal imprint is on us through these differences, and discovering, accepting, embracing and cooperating with God in cultivating and refining our male-specific or female-specific characteristics in this way is one of the most important life tasks facing us as men or women—especially if we are married.

The all-too-familiar feminist critique of this biblical truth is based on the idea that it condones the subjugation and potentially the exploitation of women in marriage. What such a critique misses is the fact that the man's role in the marriage, as "head" over the wife, is in fact not for his benefit primarily or any license whatsoever to abuse that responsibility, but rather this headship is carried out in a spirit and a mindset of sacrificial love for the wife and the children, with the voluntary sacrificial death of Jesus on the cross for his people—the church—always in view, calling on the man to set aside his own personal desires and priorities for the benefit of his wife and children if they have them. This usually requires the husband giving up cherished activities or hobbies and dedicating himself to the provision, protection and nurture of his wife and children, whether he likes the process of doing so or not. Likewise, just as the husband must unconditionally and sacrificially *love* the wife, the wife must unconditionally and sacrificially *respect and submit* to the leadership of the husband—not just tolerate it, but actively support and encourage it in every way she can. There must be a mutuality and a reciprocity in the spiritual, emotional and mental dynamics of marriage for it to work and bear good fruit as it was designed to. Having one person do this unilaterally is better than neither, though is not only difficult but runs a high risk of failure in the long run. It is far, far better for both husband and wife to embrace these roles and attitudes as so clearly and benevolently outlined in scripture.

God, having created both men and women, knows their design intimately and purposes good for them and their children. Consequently, his word on the subject is the most beneficial, helpful and loving possible guidance available on this most important matter. As I have struggled to align my thinking and actions with these truths, I have found that there has been a great release of blessing and harmony and peace in our marriage, and the changes are undeniable. All the credit for this needs to be given to God and the word of God that has become the supreme guide for our marriage. Matthew 7:24-27 has the most obvious applicability to marriage, because marriage is so extraordinarily important and so demanding (at least to do well), especially in the current era of self-gratification and confusion in the areas of sexuality, gender identity and so forth.

Please do not miss the latter point, as it would be impossible to overstate its significance. In fact, I do not think it would be an exaggeration to say that marriage represents the single most important area for application of the "be a rock" paradigm in all of life—with parenting being a close second. In fact, what has become clear to me from my own experience, and both observing and being subjected to our culture since my early childhood in the 1960's, is that it really isn't that hard to understand why the divorce rate of about 50% (itself a scandalous indicator of societal failure) is so astronomically high, probably unprecedented in all of human history: the rejection of God's purposes and will for marriage, and instead embracing values which are radically contrary to God's values for sexuality and marriage. If there there is one area of life where we need to stand firmly grounded on The Rock to succeed, it is in marriage. Moreover, I believe marriage is the ultimate refining furnace for character formation—an opportunity we will miss entirely if we resort to divorce (for anything short of infidelity or desertion). One final but important point before sharing two illustrations on this subject. It needs to be noted that if only one person in a marriage has the faith and willingness to obey God's will for marriage and their role in it, and is given the grace to actually do so, the marriage dynamics can and should markedly improve, and both the spouse and children will be blessed (even if they do not embrace your perspective). However, the full potential for every marriage will never really be achieved (in fact, far from it) unless both parties in the marriage are willingly following God's model for the roles of husband and wife and truly share the larger perspective by faith of the Lord's reign and rule over it. So having one person doing so is better than none, but having both doing so is infinitely better and releases unimaginable blessing and flourishing for husband, wife, children and others.

An excellent illustration of these truths would be the story of a man I heard about through a sermon at church where he was presented as an example of faithful commitment and perseverance. The story was that the lawyer who did all the legal work for the church while it was getting started had a wife who suffered from severe multiple sclerosis, to the point that she had been completely disabled for 25 years at that time. The husband not only took care of all of her needs, including feeding her, bathing her, helping her on and off the toilet, and all other activities of daily living, he also had to do all the cooking, cleaning, laundry, maintenance, bills, on top of working a full-time career as a lawyer. As was related by the pastor, he never complained or grumbled once about his situation, even though it was an unusually difficult and irreversible one. On top of the extreme difficulties on him personally, he also had the emotional strain of seeing his wife, who he obviously loved, suffering in this way. When the pastor asked the man how he did it, he said that he had made up his mind never to compare his situation to those of anyone else, but only to look at his own situation as God's will for him and accept it as such—that was the key to his ability to stay committed, supportive and honorable without any bitterness, resentment or self-pity. He recognized that what mattered most was not what his circumstances were, but what he did in response to them, how he treated his wife, how he lived out this extremely challenging reality day to day. How was he able to adopt and consistently maintain this unusual perspective for the benefit of his wife? By his faith and the word of God, which clearly spells out God's standards for married men and women—in the case the husband, to love his wife unconditionally and sacrificially, as Christ loved the church and gave himself up (in suffering and death) for her (the church). (Ephesians 5:25, 5:28, 5:32, 5:33). He recognized and embraced the reality that marriage is a sacred, covenantal relationship and that, as his marriage vows said, was "for better or worse, for richer or for poorer, in sickness and in health, until we are parted by death." How radically different—and superior—is such an example to us than that which our culture generally tolerates, expects and often encourages? Obviously this man was a very solid "rock" for his wife, not just for a time, or under favorable conditions, but permanently and under all conditions, even the most adverse ones. As a result of his faithfulness and rock-like stability and commitment to his marriage, he has not only blessed all who know him personally, but many others whose faith and desire to be a rock in their own lives will be strengthened by his example.

Another example of the "be a rock" principle in marriage is illustrated in the story of a man I know personally. I will call him Steve and his wife Mary for purposes of this account. Steve was a physician who had been working as a medical director at a big health system until he was "reorganized" out of a job. His efforts to find another job proved fruitless, in part because of his wife's unwillingness to move. His wife was running a successful landscaping business at the time and they had a 7 year old daughter, so Steve adapted the new situation to being a stay-at-home dad who did not have a job outside the home. Three years into this arrangement, his wife unexpectedly announced she wanted a divorce, after 16 years of marriage. Although she initiated divorce proceedings at that time, Steve fought this effort vigorously, believing that marriage is a life-long commitment with significant implications, in the context of which he strongly believed it was not God's will for their marriage to end. His faith was bolstered by dreams and a vision, which prophesied restoration. Unfortunately, Mary was not receptive to this perspective and pursued the divorce relentlessly. Steve had become a Christian about 1 year before these events began to unfold and reached out to other men and women of God for support. He did receive significant and instrumental support in many ways and from a number of people, including the lawyer who represented him who was himself a Messianic Jew (Christian with a Jewish background) and provided not only the critical legal help but some very wise and godly counsel. Not everyone, however, shared Steve's faith in restoration. Even his own pastor was acquiescent. This response from his home church led Steve on a spiritual odyssey throughout many churches in his area, growing in God's truth and grace. Despite Steve's efforts, the divorce went through. His now ex-wife became involved in an adulterous relationship. This relationship continued for a couple of years thereafter. Over the 2 years after the divorce was finalized, Mary became mentally ill and suicidal, requiring psychiatric hospitalization three times during that interval. Steve felt moved, despite his wife's actions toward him and their marriage in recent years, to support her and be as helpful and caring as possible to her, particularly when she was acutely unstable mentally. He even visited her in the psychiatric hospital. Then Mary had a change of heart and indicated her desire to reconcile with Steve. Over the next couple of years, and with counseling, they were able to fully reconcile and even remarried. A few years later, Mary was stricken with breast cancer which was, as Steve put it, a major "wake-up call" for her, after which she began to pursue her Christian faith seriously for the first time. Their shared faith was an important part of the gradual healing of their marriage. Their daughter (who came to a saving faith in Jesus Christ during the crisis) and grandchildren have been greatly blessed through this process. For me, this is a dramatic and counter-cultural story of redemption which was made possible by Steve's strong faith, his reliance on the word of God and the promises and commands therein, and the apparent direct action of a loving, merciful God on Mary to turn her heart back to her husband and eventually back to God. Steve was clearly a remarkable "rock" for Mary—and ultimately their daughter—through this ordeal, but of course Steve, in and of himself, readily admits he was completely lacking in the necessary stability, substance or resources to rise to such a massive challenge. In fact, as he readily acknowledged to me, his radical resolve to restore the marriage, driven by the belief it was God's will, came out of a lot of brokenness and failure on his part. He gives all the credit to God for making his (God's) strength perfect in Steve's extreme weakness for significant redemptive purposes. His capacity to be a rock in such an extended and personal crisis was solely a function of his standing on the word of God and his faith in God and His promises. From that foundation and perspective, he knew all things were possible and that God hates divorce, and he had the faith and patience to see a great miracle occur not only in their marriage but in Mary's mind and heart as well. Furthermore, God's miraculous restoration also extended dramatically to Steve's career and family finances. Steve's story has also been a blessing to me and many others who have heard it. There can be no denying the goodness, mercy, grace, deliverance and healing power of God in a situation such as this, who is due all the thanks and glory for it.

Being a Rock as a Parent

The scriptural revelation on the subject of parenting is significant though somewhat less clear or straightforward than that on marriage, at least to me. This may be in part because parenting is more open-ended and involves more variability than does the approach to marriage. In light of this reality, a good starting point would be to review some key scriptures on the subject:

Honor your father and your mother, that your days may be long in the land that the LORD *your God is giving you.* (Exodus 20:12)

Train up a child in the way he should go; even when he is old he will not depart from it. (Proverbs 22:6)

Fathers, do not provoke your children to anger, but bring them up in the discipline and instruction of the Lord. (Ephesians 6:4)

And these words that I command you today shall be on your heart. You shall teach them diligently to your children, and shall talk of them when you sit in your house, and when you walk by the way, and when you lie down, and when you rise. (Deuteronomy 6:6-7)

Blessed is everyone who fears the LORD, who walks in his ways! You shall eat the fruit of the labor of your hands; you shall be blessed, and it shall be well with you. Your wife will be like a fruitful vine within your house; your children will be like olive shoots around your table. Behold, thus shall the man be blessed who fears the LORD. (Psalm 128:1-4)

And he will turn the hearts of fathers to their children and the hearts of children to their fathers, lest I come and strike the land with a decree of utter destruction. (Malachi 4:6)

Then children were brought to him that he might lay his hands on them and pray. The disciples rebuked the people, but Jesus said, "Let the little children come to me and do not hinder them, for to such belongs the kingdom of heaven." And he laid his hands on them and went away. (Matthew 19:13-15)

Children, obey your parents in the Lord, for this is right. "Honor your father and mother" (this is the first commandment with a promise), "that it may go well with you and that you may live long in the land." Fathers, do not provoke your children to anger, but bring them up in the discipline and instruction of the Lord. (Ephesians 6:1-4)

The Bible has more to say regarding parenting, but these verses represent a core selection which I believe capture the essence of the biblical perspective on parenting and have large implications which confirm and correspond to the main thesis of this book. First, it is clear throughout scripture that God has a high view and significant purposes for the family and cares very much for the "little ones" who are vulnerable and dependent not only on their parents but on God. God is faithful in this arrangement, but are we? As parents, we are all accountable to God for our stewardship and leadership of our children. This is a most significant and weighty, though also joyful and rich, responsibility. Parents, both father and mother need to "be a rock" for their children. This begins with our own integrity and stability derived from being grounded in the truth and by having cultivated our relationship with and knowledge of God such that we are firmly rooted and established on the Rock which does not change and is able to supply our every need, in every dimension of life. This enables us to then both unconditionally love as well as provide for (materially, emotionally, spiritually) our children's needs, and their needs are very significant. In fact, for me, this may be the most difficult section of this book to write. Of all the many ways God has shown me that I have failed and fallen short, none has grieved—or, frankly, appalled—me as much as my shortcomings in this domain of responsibility. While I no doubt could have done a worse job as a father, and there were probably a number of things I did reasonably well, when belatedly came to more fully understand God's purposes and basic blueprint for parenting, it was a shocking revelation of the real magnitude of my shortcomings in this most weighty domain of responsibility. Which values and principles do we rely on to guide us as parents—our culture's (or the world's), or God's? From my experience and my knowledge of God's word, the mindset of the former is of personal achievement, success and security, while that of the latter is of faithfulness to God and responding to his will for me. These two approaches to this most important undertaking could not be more different, with profound implications for the spiritual well-being of our children. My purpose here is not to instill a sense of guilt in parents, since none are perfect and all have fallen short in one way or another. The point here is to recognize the critical role we as parents play in the development of our children. We do not do this in a vacuum but recognize that we are accountable to God for our children and their management by us. We need a lot of help for this hugely challenging undertaking, but God has provided that help in his word, the Bible, and through a personal relationship with him and with the help of the Holy Spirit, who as

Jesus taught his disciples would "teach you all things and bring to remembrance all that I have said to you." (John 14:26) Perhaps the most important responsibility of all for a parent is to pray for our children—but this will be effective only if we ourselves are grounded and founded on the Rock. Just taking our children to church, even having them participate in mission trips or other church-related youth activities, may be good and potentially transformative, but our responsibility as parents is to model the life of faith and obedience to God by actually living it out, as imperfectly as we all do.

Being a Rock in our Work Life

The principles being advocated in this book also apply in the domain of work. If you are a son or daughter of the Most High God, you have a special opportunity and responsibility to perform with excellence, integrity, honor and with a selfless work ethic for the benefit of your clientele, your colleagues, and the watching world. You are in a position to demonstrate such qualities of character and thereby bless those with whom you work but also will set an example for others on the meaning of excellence in the workplace. When you consistently demonstrate that your main motivation is not to benefit yourself but to honor and glorify God, over time people will tend to take note and either be intrigued by what makes you tick—giving you an opportunity to share your faith—or at least be convicted of any shortcomings they may have in that area of endeavor, hopefully resulting in improvements in their working habits and ethics.

Scripture does speak to the importance of this issue. In Colossians 3:23-24, Paul writes: *Whatever you do, work heartily as for the Lord and not for men, knowing that from the Lord you will receive the inheritance as your reward. You are serving the Lord Christ.* There are also several verses in Proverbs exhorting the reader to be diligent and industrious in work, with warnings for those who are lazy and slothful. To share a bit of my personal story with regard to this point, for a variety of reasons including the unusually demanding nature of the work I do as a nephrologist, in recent years I had found myself getting into a bit of a rut, feeling a growing sense of possible burnout and perhaps a touch of bitterness that was not healthy or conducive to my best possible performance in my professional responsibilities. More recently I have found that my attitude and energy levels and commitment to excellence in my work has greatly improved, which I attribute to a combination of specific and increasingly persistent prayer that this would be the case, and also to an experience of having a day off a week for a period of several months which I felt led of the Lord to do. After a while and that arrangement started to realize that I wanted to be working more full-time, and I was able to go back to a full schedule with renewed appreciation for the special kind of work that God has given me to do. I consider it an honor as well as a responsibility to have such meaningful work. I'm appreciating more and more the intellectual aspects of it that are keeping my mind sharp and giving me a level of knowledge and expertise that is also a privilege. Most of all, I believe it is a way of serving God to do all that I can to provide the most excellent medical care to my patients and to be flexible to help out and make an effort to communicate effectively with my colleagues within the practice and outside of it. I find that doing so is an important component of staying in God's will for my life, as from God's perspective there is really no compartmentalization of the different areas of our lives such as work, recreation, relationships, family, and religion/spirituality. When God is truly Lord of your life, *everything* comes under his reign and rule and should be done for his glory, and I have found that embracing this perspective in the domain of my work has been enormously beneficial to myself, my patients, my colleagues and even my family.

Being a Rock in Our Faith

For the person of faith, our journey of life in this world will be characterized by endless assaults (directly or indirectly) on the foundation of our beliefs and therefore of our life. We can not be naive and expect everything to be smooth sailing after committing our lives to Christ and living out our faith in a fallen world. The Bible takes it a step further than that in realistically portraying the level of opposition to obeying God any believer will face at various points when it reveals that the devil, that is Satan, is the "prince of the power of the air" (Ephesians 2:2) and the "ruler of this world" (John 12:31, John 14:30, John 16:11). To me, this truth has become increasingly evident in the current times and, if anything, more important than ever for the people of God to understand. If the world is run by a fallen humanity, and if the devil is the "ruler of this world," to which fallen humanity is subject, how easy do we expect it to be to keep on track with our faith and our life, even if we embrace the Christian faith with commitment and zeal? Unfortunately, in my experience, this is exceedingly difficult—though definitely possible—and requires a high level of commitment. Such total commitment to following Christ as the only mediator and advocate between God and man is not a light or casual matter. It is, in the end, an all-or-nothing proposition. To think we can have God (fully and securely) and also have the world (with all of its false promises and pseudo-security) is folly as well as unbiblical. Further, to think we will be able to "get along famously" with the world and all (or most) people while still following Christ and obeying God is also unrealistsic and, like it or not, contrary to the teaching of scripture. It is important to note that the lack of harmony between God's people and a fallen world is a result of the latter's opposition to God's reign and rule, and God clearly calls his people to respond to this reality with the truth, but to do so in love and with a willingness to forgive, compassion, and gentleness. We are to be blameless in this matter while offering the only saving truth, in love, to a lost and dying world. While scripture is clear that Jesus Christ has overcome the fallen world, the tyranny of the flesh (our carnal nature) over our lives, and our supernatural adversary the devil, these three factors continue to operate in the world and in our lives to the extent that God allows it even after we surrender to him and commit to follow Jesus. This results in difficult tradeoffs we will face in our life of faith, ones which may require us to sacrifice something precious to us in order for God's will to be done in our lives. It may make some of us quite uncomfortable to think that we may lose some of our most valued "assets" in the process, but from a biblical perspective (and therefore God's), what we give up in this world can not be compared to the inestimable value of that which we gain through faith and obedience to Christ.

An illustration from my own faith journey is directly relevant to this point. I was a very active and involved member of a men-only organization designed to promote friendships within a Christian context which operated through local chapters nationwide. I found the combination of friendships and faith this group provided to be extremely compelling and enjoyable, attending the annual national and regional retreats and getting involved in leadership activity. Some close friendships were formed, and my faith was definitely enriched for a time. The model and purpose of this involvement met a significant need and became quite precious to me. However, after about five years of heavy engagement with the organization, key members of the national and regional leadership became enamored of the book, The Shack, and its author, Paul Young. So much so that Young was made one of the main speakers at the past two national retreats and then in late 2017 was chosen to be the "spiritual guide" for the much more intimate but still well-attended northeast regional retreat. In addition, at the last national retreat, a big push (and obvious expense) was made by the leadership to showcase the movie based on the book, chartering a bus to view the movie pre-release in Washington, and sending out a video to all the membership shortly before the conference was to start, in which the organization's president enthusiastically endorsed the movie event for all attendees. None of this would have been a real problem for me had the book and movie been based on what I would consider sound theology. I'd heard about the book a number of years before, and what I'd read about it back then had given me concerns about the theological perspective presented by the book, though I hadn't read it at that point. The more I heard of it through trusted sources, the less I wanted to read the book, but I eventually did because I knew that if I was going to challenge the leadership on their increasing infatuation with The Shack, I would at least have to read it, which I then did, carefully and thoughtfully; I also read more articles as well as a book by a biblical scholar and seminary professor who had a close personal relationship with Young during the years leading up to and immediately following his publishing of The Shack which he skillfully critiqued from a conservative (or in other words biblical) theological perspective. I also heard Paul Young's personal testimony in person twice (at the national retreats) and watched other interviews with him on Youtube to be sure I understood his theological perspective. While the issues and doctrines raised in this process were complex and his personal story evoked great empathy and a recognition of his brokenness, it only became clearer to me on further evaluation that there were major problems with the theology presented in the book. I suspect that this was, at least in part, a result of his traumatic experiences as a child under various forms of serious abuse as well as a highly flawed approach to the Christian faith modeled by his missionary parents and later exacerbated by his own personal crises followed by extensive psychotherapy. I have real compassion for this sincere, no doubt brilliant, and earnest man (who I have also met personally at their national events), and I'll acknowledge that many people believe the book has helped them better understand and be more comfortable with God than they had ever been previously. However, when it comes to the revealed truth of God, there can be no "giving a pass" to flawed theology on account of of tragic or traumatic personal histories on the part of those disseminating that theology. The God of the Bible is by nature deeply relational and loving and knowing Him is a profoundly personal experience, but it *can never be at the expense of altering the truth* He has revealed about Himself or about us.

The final result of these developments was that after much thought and prayer, I questioned the key leadership of the organization about their aggressive promotion of the book through the platform they had in this national men's group, and the response was unfortunately, to politely defend both Young and The Shack, rather than to seriously consider my perspective. Although by that point I certainly was not surprised by this response, nevertheless this was particularly hard for me as I was quite fond of all 3 of these men, and rather close to one of them in particular, and had developed other strong friendships through the group. Despite the close relationships, enjoyable events, and other benefits of my involvement with this organization, I eventually came to the difficult conclusion that I had no choice but to dissociate from it, as I felt my ability to remain faithful to God would inevitably be compromised if I continued in it. That may not be the case for others involved in that organization, who are at different places in their faith journey, but it was for me, and since making that decision, I have had no real misgivings about it, although it was painful and, in a sense, heartbreaking for me personally. The reason I am sharing this part of my story is *not* to criticize this group of men (which I have chosen not to identify by name for that reason), rather to point out that the level of commitment to the truth I'm trying to share in this book will inevitably require changes in your life, but seen in the right perspective, these changes are good and necessary and in the final analysis will bring greater blessings than anything which might have been sacrificed for the sake of loyalty to Jesus Christ. In my life of faith there have been a few critical points where I had to surrender something very precious to me in obedience to God—sometimes that which had captivated my heart most at that particular point. Each such experience was painful, sometimes scary, and required difficult adjustments, but each led me to much greater freedom and ultimately strengthened my faith. Such pivotal moments are an unavoidable and healthy component of our transformation into the sons and daughter of God he is calling us to become, and although we may not realize it at the time, we will be thankful for the providential and benevolent guidance of God through such experiences.

The subject of how to be a rock in every key domain of life is far too big to be handled in this chapter, but hopefully you can get a flavor for such applications in the foregoing sections. Another way to put flesh on this insight is to briefly explore some real life people who exemplify this principle of being a rock under adverse conditions.

Case studies of Real-World Rocks

These few historical and biblical case studies are being presented to illustrate the main point of this book, that one individual can develop and consistently operate out of a level of character which can have significant and lasting impact for good in the lives of others. This is especially true in those areas of life that are most strategically important, in whatever circumstances in which they find themselves.

My first example of a real life "rock" is the biblical figure of Joseph, the son of Jacob, who was the grandson of Abraham, universally recognized as the patriarch of the 3 major monotheistic religions of the world (Judaism, Christianity, and Islam). Jacob married Rachael (out of love) and her sister Leah (as a result of the deception of their father) and Rachael was unable to have children until very late in life, when she had her first child, Joseph. Jacob favored Joseph because he was born to Rachel in their old age against all the laws of nature, and this favoritism was apparent to the 10 older brothers who became jealous and eventually sold him into slavery in Egypt. Because of his integrity and faithfulness to the God of his fathers even in the pagan land of Egypt, he consistently refused the seductive overtures of the wife of his master, over whose household he had been entrusted with complete authority because of his unusual competence and trustworthiness. When the wife could not seduce him, she accused him of trying to sexually assault her, a brazen lie but enough to get Joseph locked up in prison for years. While in prison he interpreted (by revelation of God) the dreams of Pharaoh's baker and chief cup-bearer, and eventually the cup-bearer remembered Joseph's ability to interpret dreams when Pharaoh had a dream which Pharaoh knew was extremely important but which no one, including all the wise men, astrologers and magicians of the land, could interpret. Joseph interpreted the dream perfectly, which predicted 7 years of plentiful harvests to be followed by 7 years of severe famine, and he provided wise counsel as to what to do about this future crisis. Pharaoh immediately recognized Joseph's unusual qualities including wisdom and integrity (and the fact that "the spirit of God" was in him) and made him second in command over all Egypt after only Pharaoh himself. (Genesis 41:38) In that role, Joseph masterfully managed the entire country and no doubt saved many millions of people from starvation and very possibly even the Egyptian empire from collapsing and being overrun by rival empires. Joseph's entire family moved to Egypt to ride out the famine, and in the process established the the Jewish people as a large group with a distinctive identity and heritage, which ultimately became the nation of Israel, which eventually also produced the Old Testament and the setting into which the Messiah appeared, as extensively prophesied by scripture, for the salvation of humanity. The main point here is that if Joseph had succumbed to the overtures of the adulterous wife of his master, there is no way to know what would have become of Joseph, but you can be sure he would not have ended up saving Egypt and much of the ancient world, nor provided the ideal incubator for the people of God—the Jews—to grow into a nation from which would ultimately come the world's savior and the holy scriptures. Clearly his competence, integrity, reliability, trustworthiness, and wisdom were such that he was able to do the supremely difficult job he did to save Egypt, and this was done as a believer in the God of Abraham, Isaac and Jacob while living at the zenith of a deeply pagan society. The accomplishment is awe-inspiring, but the important insight here is that all of Joseph's fine qualities and gifts were all from God and were informed by his knowledge of, and dependence on, God, a fact he would have readily acknowledged if asked. This is clear in his response to Pharaoh's high compliment to Joseph at the beginning of their first interaction, to which Joseph replied, "*It is not in me.* God will give Pharaoh a favorable answer." (Genesis 41:16; emphasis added) As giant a historical figure as he is, he would never have had any impact or been known as he is had it not been for the truth, grace, help, wisdom and power that only God could supply him, as well as his own faithfulness to God in response.

Another figure in the Bible is Esther, a young woman who was a Jewish orphan living in the capital of the ancient Persian empire in the fifth century, B.C., and being raised by her uncle, Mordecai. Through an unusual sequence of events, she became queen to King Ahasureus (also known as Xerxes I) who reigned over the whole Persian empire. While queen, Esther learned of a plot devised by the second in command in the empire, Haman, to completely exterminate the Jewish people, a plan Haman devised after being insulted by the lack of deferential flattering he expected from Mordecai. Because of Esther's faith and the related wisdom and courage to address this plot with the king (which she risked her life to do), she was able to completely avert the plot and turn the tables on those who sought to destroy the Jews, themselves ultimately being destroyed. From that time on, the Jews were held in especially high esteem by the surrounding culture, even though they did not presumably (or at least generally) recognize or fear the God of the Jews, all as a result of Esther's capacity to stand strong in the crisis—all of which was in turn by the knowledge, grace and power of God.

A third biblical figure, and a special case in this regard, is the apostle Peter. Peter was known for his impetuousness and lack of reliability at various key points during the earthly ministry of Jesus. At one point after Jesus had performed a miracle involving fish, Peter, recognizing he was in the presence of true greatness and holiness, in response asked Jesus to "depart from me, for I am a sinful man." He was later rebuked by Jesus for being an agent of Satan at a critical moment in Jesus' ministry when he revealed God's plan for him to be captured, tortured and executed. Peter also argued with Jesus about letting Jesus wash his feet at the last supper, thinking he had a better way to do it that Jesus did. He even drew his sword and cut off the ear of the high priest's servant when they were arresting Jesus in direct violation of Jesus' clear instructions and the Father's will, much akin to the earlier episode where he opposed God's will for Jesus. He denied even knowing Jesus three times in the courtyard after Jesus was captured and while he was being interrogated. In spite of all this, Jesus seems to call him a rock in Matthew 16:18: *And I tell you, you are Peter, and on this rock I will build my church, and the gates of hell shall not prevail against it.* The obvious question here is, how could Jesus, who is the true Rock, have bestowed such a high honor and distinction on Peter, singling him out as being a "rock" upon which he would build his church, when he was clearly so unstable and fickle, not to mention unwilling to submit to God's express will? It is very clear from what we know of him in the pages of scripture that, overall, Peter was anything but a rock during Jesus' earthly ministry. After much thought and evaluation of the surrounding text and other parts of scripture that speak to these issues—particularly with Matthew 7:24-27 in mind—I believe that Jesus was referring to the *declaration by Peter* of the identity of Jesus as the Messiah, the statement of this ultimate truth, that is the real "rock" in view here. Peter in and of himself was certainly no "rock," at least at that point, but he would later become one because of the truth he had just uttered, as it more fully penetrated his mind and heart and he became yielded to God's will for him, a transition which occurred dramatically in Acts chapter 2 with Pentecost and the pouring out of the Holy Spirit on all those who were gathered in the upper room that day. From that day forward, Peter became extremely bold as was seen in the Pentecost story as well as his dramatic confrontation shortly thereafter with the ruling religious authorities (in Acts chapter 3), the same ones who had ensured Jesus would be crucified only weeks before. From that point forward, Peter's ministry was marked with supernatural power, miracles, the writing of two magnificent and important epistles in the canon of the New Testament, and ultimately bringing glory to the Lord by being martyred for his faith, being crucified head-down according to tradition. Perhaps more than any other character in the pages of the Bible, Peter is so relatable to us in our weakness and failures, yet God was able to make him into one of the greatest "rocks" of the Christian faith, so he can do similarly with us.

Questions for reflection:

1. Do you believe you are being the "rock" you could be in your marriage and as a parent? If not, how could you move in that direction?

2. Have you ever given up an important relationship or affiliation for the sake of your relationship with God? If not, can you think of any connection/affiliation in your life which impedes your effectiveness in being the "rock" you were designed and are being called to be?

3. Do you think Joseph could have become the epic "rock" he was in ancient Egypt and for the people of Israel if he had not done what was difficult but right with regard to the incident with Potiphar's wife?

4. Which sources or practices provide us with the strength, wisdom and courage to overcome our natural flaws to operate as the most stable, reliable, helpful and honorable people we were made to be?

Chapter 8
Approaching the Bible and Choosing a Church

Among those who embrace the Christian faith, the serious practitioner will be faced, sooner or later, with an important fundamental decision point of great significance. There are many denominations falling under the general umbrella of "Christianity." The exact number is debatable, possibly in the thousands worldwide (depending on how you define a denomination), but the point is there are so many versions of churches with a "Christian" label as to confuse anyone who does not have a clear and informed approach to evaluating not only the denominations but individual churches, whether independent or not. This situation presents a bewildering range of options for church affiliation. I recognize that many people may already feel committed to a particular type of church, for whatever reason, and not even have considered the possibility that there may be better—much better perhaps—churches out there. Regardless, I believe this discussion is as important for folks in this category as for those who are not yet firmly attached to any one church or brand of Christianity.

My perspective on this topic is that you and I are actually 100% free to choose the very best church possible for us (even if it doesn't seem that way at first). Not only are we at liberty to do so, it is imperative that we do so for our spiritual health and effectiveness in life. In fact, I believe that God himself is intimately and actively interested in your own spiritual growth, and consequently in which church you engage with. It is most definitely not a simple matter of preferences based on the sociodemographic profile of the members, the quality of the worship music, how charismatic (with regard to preaching style) the pastor is, or the appearance/location/characteristics of the church building. I'm quite sure that none of that is of much (if any) importance to God, and hence if we are to "be a rock" in this most critical area of life, neither can any of these factors be very important to us. What needs to be prioritized above all else in choosing a church is this: finding the most biblically-faithful and Holy Spirit-filled church possible, with stylistic/aesthetic/sociodemographic factors taking a back seat to these primary considerations. The question of which church to attend is, I believe, one of the most important decisions you will make in your entire life. While this decision is not irrevocable and binding as it is in choosing who to marry, it carries enormous implications for your spiritual growth and hence in your long-term effectiveness in the most important domains of life.

Thankfully, after many years of groping in the dark on this question, I have come to recognize what I consider to be the single most important metric to evaluate the potential validity and quality of any church. This metric does not tell the whole story for any given church, but it can, in my opinion, eliminate many (and I suspect most) churches from consideration, narrowing the options greatly, which in the case of church selection is very helpful. The key to this process of discernment it to recognize that there is one great dividing line that cuts across all doctrinal, geographical, cultural, and stylistic differences, resulting in two great overarching "camps" that all churches fall into. I am intimately familiar with both camps, having spent most of my adult life as a Christian in one camp, but I am now firmly in the other. I will readily admit that there are some nuances and shades of differences which may not easily be accounted for by this approach, and that I am neither as qualified nor as prepared as some are to elaborate on this point, but I'm convinced of the truth of this observation and believe it can serve us well as the core metric by which we evaluate any church or organization or belief system which claims to be Christian in nature. There are books out there which explain the differences and historical background of all the major denominations, and that is well beyond the scope of this book, but without a valid paradigm by which to sort all that information out, such research may not be helpful in this process anyway.

The great invisible dividing line in the Christian faith to which I am referring comes down to how we regard and approach the Bible. The first such "camp" we will discuss (though not the first historically) regards the Biblical writings as being in some general and limited sense inspired, yet imperfect and relative in its applicability. This camp points to the fact that imperfect human beings did the writing, and they consequently reason that scripture must likewise be flawed. This faction would also be inclined to embrace a paradigm in which the religious experience is subjective rather than an encounter with objective, absolute truth from God. This perspective also tends to regard the Bible (and therefore God) as having undergone a kind of "evolution" from the Old Testament to the New, and tends to perceive a disconnect between the values and perspectives of Moses and the other authors of the Old Testament on the one hand, and Jesus Christ and the writers of the New Testament books on the other. Many such folks would also point out what they perceive as discrepancies between the words (or at least the perceived messages) of Jesus Christ and those of the various New Testament writers.

The second "camp" referred to above has its roots in the earliest church is the one which is clearly growing most rapidly throughout the world. This camp regards the Bible, the 66 canonical books of the Old and New Testaments, as divinely inspired, infallible, inerrant (in the original texts), definitive, and the complete and final written revelation of God which in his sovereign wisdom and mercy he willed for humanity to have. This perspective essentially believes every verse in the Bible was directly inspired by God and is fully reliable and the ultimate reference in all matters of faith and practice (in other words, of life). One verse which speaks especially clearly to this, and represents the overall perspective throughout scripture about itself, is the following:

All scripture is given by inspiration of God, and is profitable for doctrine, for reproof, for correction, for instruction in righteousness, that the man of God may be complete, thoroughly equipped for every good work. (2 Timothy 3:16-17).

There are many other places in scripture which attest to the same perspective on its authority, and it is clear that Jesus Christ himself fully embraced this perspective (see John 10:35). Each person seeking an accurate knowledge of God must come to terms with this issue. One cannot have it both ways. Either the Bible is the infallible and unchanging word of God Himself, divinely produced from beginning to end (as well articulated in the Chicago Statement cited in Chapter 4 above), or it is something else. One problem with the latter relativistic approach to the Bible is that it makes *us* the judge of Scripture. It actually exalts human wisdom over that of God. And if God didn't directly craft all biblical scripture, then what parts of it can we trust as true? Here's the point: if we won't trust it as true in its entirety, we are inevitably elevating human wisdom over God's revelation. How much sense does that make? Of course, it doesn't, but even if one thinks it does, one thing is clear—it contradicts the biblical perspective. So one cannot, on the one hand, claim to follow the Bible as the ultimate source of God's truth and at the same time hold to a relativistic, man-centered theology that demotes the authority of the Bible to a level below ours.

Origins of Liberal Christian Theology

It is worthwhile to briefly note the role of two historical figures, one of whom specifically was instrumental in the shift of perspective away from biblical authority which came eventually to be embraced by what appears to be a majority of churches that have historically been Christian and are still labeled as such, along with the majority of individuals associated with such churches. To set the stage for the latter, the Enlightenment of the 18th century eventually came to have a huge influence on subsequent theological thought. Immanuel Kant, a German philosopher in the late 1700's, was instrumental in ushering in a change in the very understanding of our perception of reality which was a central part of Enlightenment thought. His self-proclaimed "Copernican revolution" of how we apprehend external reality presented a paradigm which posits that we cannot know the external reality we observe because our perceptions, in essence, cannot be trusted. This had the ultimate effect of elevating the place of man relative to any theological knowledge and raising questions about the reliability of the latter. As Kant was gaining widespread popularity, the major figure regarded as the "father of modern theological liberalism" emerged: Friederich Schleiermacher, a German theologian who lived in the late 1700's-early 1800's (ESV Study Bible, p. 2618). Schleiermacher was deeply influenced by the philosophy of Kant. He applied the same shift in perspective to the study of God as Kant did in the realm of thought, with the net effect being to teach that we cannot know God as he really is, but can only reliably "know" our own personal experience of God. The emphasis morphed from the knowledge of God through his direct revelation in the Bible and in history, toward a predominantly (if not entirely) subjective experience, to the point that the latter largely replaced the former. From this perspective the Bible loses its authority as the direct written revelation of God and becomes an account of the allegedly subjective experiences of various people at different times in history, all subject to our own interpretation and to be used as seems fitting or helpful. Not only the biblical teaching on such subjects as moral truth were now questioned, but even the historical accounts of key events in the Bible were considered doubtful, including events of such central importance to the Christian faith as the virgin birth of Jesus Christ and his resurrection. The significance of this shift in the view of biblical authority would be hard to overstate, as it eventually took root in many, if not most, of the major Protestant denominations throughout the world, embracing a radically altered view of scripture which negates and undermines its authority. This theologically liberal perspective has even set in so deeply at most seminaries identifying themselves as Christian that, in general, it is nearly impossible for anyone who fully embraces the biblical account of creation or the exodus or the events surrounding the birth, death and resurrection of Jesus Christ, or the numerous miracles recorded in the New Testament to be hired to teach there, no matter how outstanding their academic credentials and personal character may be. This is a discouraging state of affairs but should not be surprising to anyone familiar with the worldview presented by the Bible. Generally speaking, I believe there are far too many seminaries for the numbers of people who are genuinely called by God to undertake graduate level theological education, and like other forms of higher education, it is ultimately a business which has a will to survive and will readily compromise and abandon biblical authority (assuming they ever really embraced it in the first place) unless it is steadfastly and unapologetically committed to biblical authority, having counted the cost of doing so, and would rather go out of business or struggle to survive than be unfaithful to the God they serve and love above everything the world can offer.

In the current era, there is one particularly glaring example of the degree to which this relativistic perspective on the authority and applicability of the Bible, both Old and New Testament, is impacting the "church." This has to do with the belief that the standard for sexual morality has "evolved" from the perspective presented by the Bible to something entirely different. The biblical perspective on sexuality may be a difficult one to consider for the modern person, but it is clear and consistent throughout: any and all sexual activity outside of marriage between one man and one woman, including adultery, premarital/extramarital sex (fornication), and homosexuality, are all prohibited and therefore fall into the category of disobedience to God (also known as sin). Such disobedience represents a rejection of God's right to determine acceptable limits for the use of this most unique and precious, but dangerous, gift of sexuality. The theologically liberal or "evolved" (as proponents of this perspective like to describe themselves) view is that the biblical standard on sexuality is no longer relevant, that human beings have "progressed" in their understanding. They raise what they consider to be a rhetorical question: how can it really be wrong for two consenting adults who love and are committed to each other to be in a sexually intimate relationship (regardless of their current or prior marital status or their genders)? The recent Supreme Court case of Masterpiece Cake Shop vs. the Colorado Civil Rights Commission puts in perspective how far our culture has migrated from generally Judeo-Christian (hence Biblical) values to the new perspective which rejects such a standard. Numerous other cases of a similar nature are being or have recently been fought out in the courts, including those of the Washington florist Barronelle Stutzman and Oregon bakers Aaron and Melissa Klein. The Supreme Court recognized the anti-Christian spirit which drove the unjust and egregiously punitive decisions against these Christians when they decided in favor of Masterpiece Cake Shop (7-2), but the fact that this process was stopped only at the Supreme Court level should get us all to take note of the massive shift in societal values which has occurred in our lifetime. And the battle only seems to be intensifying, unfortunately. While this dramatic change in society's core moral values may seem to have come out of nowhere and taken hold of vast segments of the church in a matter of a few decades, the roots of this larger cultural shift can be traced to a handful of highly influential people, the most significant of which was Carl Jung. How this process was able to infiltrate the church, in turn, can be largely credited to the liberal theological revolution of Shleiermacher, followed by many others. Based on the logic of the latter, there is in fact nothing surprising about the fact that large percentages of churches have now completely rejected the biblical view of sexual morality and the binary nature of gender and embraced a sexual value set which is totally incompatible with the biblical witness—yet within the prevailing paradigm of *liberal* Protestantism, this is not only possible, it was actually inevitable and predictable. As soon as one rejects the absolute authority of the Bible as God's definitive word, they are operating under a totally different paradigm than the one by which God is actually in charge and we are but his creatures and subjects whose only concern is to understand God's will for us and to then do it. What a stark illustration this is of the extent of the implications such a shift in biblical perspective can bring about! Can anyone miss just how astonishing this progression is?

In the modern era of Christianity in America, there is an overwhelming emphasis on God's love, mercy, forgiveness and grace. This is not all bad, as these characteristics of God are important and set the God of the Bible apart from any other conception of "god." But every bit as important as these almost universally appealing aspects of God are, his his absolute (unchanging and universal) truth, his holiness, his righteousness, and ultimate judgment of all people is equally important to understand and embrace. It is spiritually hazardous to count on the former attributes of God without having equal respect and reverence for the latter ones. In fact, the Bible repeatedly emphasizes that the *fear* of God as the *beginning* of wisdom, in recognition of our fallen and spiritually depraved condition before a perfectly holy, righteous and just God. The liberal Protestantism camp doesn't just downplay those latter attributes, it largely rejects them—especially the key ones of absolute truth (or biblical authority) and of sin. Unfortunately for those who share that perspective, they are clearly at variance with the Bible in general, and Jesus specifically, who could not have been more clear in elevating a knowledge of the truth to the level of supreme importance. It's not just another facet of God's nature, but the key aspect of our relationship with God that must be dealt with and ultimately embraced fully for us to unlock and appropriate the former attributes of God's love, grace, mercy and the other benefits and blessings of a restored, right relationship with him. At this point it is of particular importance to make this point clear; it is not a stylistic or academic or theologically complicated issue of our faith to understand our true condition before God, and his true qualities and character. To get this wrong could prove disastrous. A relevant verse from scripture speaking to the question of absolute truth indicates both the unparalleled freedom and yet the high level of commitment in question:

So Jesus said to the Jews who had believed him, "If you abide in my word, you are truly my disciples, and you will know the truth, and the truth will set you free." (John 8:31-32)

In this statement, Jesus places the emphasis on "my word" just as he did in Matthew 7:24-27, indicating that his word is both the key to our freedom and a sure foundation on which to live. Not only knowing but also receiving and loving the truth is required for access to this freedom. It is not a secondary matter. The modern American church increasingly has relegated the truth, or in church parlance, "doctrine," to a subordinate level of concern for one obvious reason: to minimize controversy and friction among people, to avoid offending anyone, and to avoid losing members. The seeker-friendly megachurch phenomenon, and many significant parachurch ministries, are sacrificing a clear and unwavering commitment to the truth for the sake of a comfortable relationship with the world, because the ultimate goal (as I see it in this case) is to maximize the numbers of people attending such churches, rather than for the foremost concern being to be faithful to the revealed truth of God. As I saw in my experience with the Christian men's organization I touched on previously, in general I see a level of theological compromise in liberal churches and some prominent megachurches which undermined the ability of such churches to serve as faithful witnesses to the unpopular truth of God. Along these lines, shortly after Jesus' statement about the truth setting us free in John 8:32, he identifies the origin of spiritual opposition to the truth in describing the devil this way: *"He was a murderer from the beginning, and does not stand in the truth, because there is no truth in him. When he lies, he speaks out of his own character, for he is a liar and the father of lies."* (John 8:44b) Any conscious distortion of the truth is a form of lying, and the latter verse makes it clear what the source of all lying is spiritually.

This perspective on truth is so integral throughout to the entire biblical message that it is insufficient to simply present verses to illustrate the point. It ultimately requires us to invest time in reading the Bible ourselves to verify the point I am trying to make about the supreme importance of the truth in our ability to be a rock, as well as our ability to obey God. This is because ultimately the only way we have solid ground to stand on and not be thrown off course by subtle and appealing lies is to be so grounded in the knowledge of the truth that we will be able to identify the lies and distortions when they come—and they will come with regularity. However, it is worth looking briefly at a few passages which speak to this point so we may at least begin to grapple with this issue which I believe is a much bigger one than the vast majority of people who profess to be Christians recognize in the current era:

But I have a few things against you: you have some there who hold the teaching of Balaam, who taught Balak to put a stumbling block before the sons of Israel, so that they might eat food sacrificed to idols and practice sexual immorality. So also you have some who hold the teaching of the Nicolaitans. Therefore repent. If not, I will come to you soon and war against them with the sword of my mouth. (Revelation 2:14-16)

So in addressing the first century church in Pergamum, Jesus Christ praised it with the following words: *Yet you hold fast my name, and you did not deny my faith even in the days of Antipas my faithful witness, who was killed among you, where Satan dwells.* (Revelation 2:13) Though they were willing even to die for their faith, Jesus rebukes them for holding to "the teaching of Balaam" and the "teaching of the Nicolaitans" both of which advocated licentiousness regarding what activities and behaviors are acceptable. This same theme is present in his words to other churches in the related passages.

Another verse which references the truth as a sword is Hebrews 4:12:

For the word of God is living and active, sharper than any two-edged sword, piercing to the division of soul and of spirit, of joints and of marrow, and discerning the thoughts and intentions of the heart.

Note that the sword in the foregoing verses refers to both the word of God and the Holy Spirit, as in Ephesians 6:17 which uses the language, *the sword of the Spirit, which is the word of God.* Note that in Ephesians 6 in the list of "spiritual armor" presented by Paul, the sword of the Spirit is the only offensive weapon—it penetrates and confronts darkness with light, a process which the "darkness" hates. The word of God, as the ultimate and definitive truth, is not about building consensus, maximizing church membership by making services appealing and giving people what they want, or becoming user-friendly. Rather, it is a declaration, which comes to humanity as nothing less than a command. This perspective is certainly not popular, but it is biblical. Please don't just take my word for it—I urge you to read from the source yourself and be convinced for yourself. To start, here are two verses that are notable for their clarity and simplicity with regard to this point:

The times of ignorance God overlooked, but now he commands all people everywhere to repent. (Acts 17:30)

And this is his commandment, that we believe in the name of his Son Jesus Christ... (1 John 3:23)

To take this point one step further, Jesus himself, it is clear, did have many followers, but frequently large majorities of those followers left (implying they rejected) him due to either the level of commitment required or a lack of faith to understand his teaching. Being a rock is not a matter of pleasing people or amassing a large fan base of followers and admirers or having high approval ratings. If anything, we can expect resistance and at times even hostility from the world if we are genuinely and consistently committed to the truth presented in the Bible. The divine paradox here, however, is that scripture also sets the highest possible standard of conduct (for followers of Jesus) toward all other people, such as in Jesus' statement, *But I say to you, love your enemies, and pray for those who persecute you,* (Matthew 5:44) or *You shall love your neighbor as yourself* (Matthew 22:39b). So God calls his people to simultaneously be radically faithful to the truth which God has revealed uniquely and definitively in the Bible without compromise, while also having a benevolent love toward all people, even those who hate or persecute you (and, for that matter, God!). This is impossible without God's help, but he does not ask us to do what is impossible. He actually supplies the grace and power to do so by granting the gift of the Holy Spirit to those who sincerely repent, rejecting our naturally self-centered way of living and embracing Jesus Christ as our Savior and our Lord, and being willing to pay the price in our own lives. While we must enter by the "narrow gate" and go a "hard way" to enter life (Matthew 7:13), Jesus also said, *Take my yoke upon you, and learn from me, for I am gentle and lowly in heart, and you will find rest for your souls. For my yoke is easy, and my burden is light.* (Matthew 11:29-30) We need to be willing to exchange the tyranny of the flesh, the world and the devil, with its associated comforts and worldly ease, for the freedom that comes only in Christ and in the truth he embodies and speaks.

My Personal Testimony

As has been alluded to previously, I underwent my own spiritual transformation which both taught and demonstrated to me personally the importance and enduring power of the truths discussed above. While this process is still far from complete (and will never be truly finished in this life), hopefully sharing a bit of my story will give some of the insights I've shared further clarity. Growing up, my family attended a local Episcopal church, somewhat regularly. As is standard in that church, I was baptized as an infant and went through confirmation in my early teens. Despite the exposure, I had no meaningful knowledge of God or of the Bible, nor any real faith in God. I never gave the subject enough thought to reject the Christian faith for anything else, but neither did I ever truly embrace the faith or feel a connection to God in those early years. I was generally a well-behaved and low-maintenance child but became increasingly self-centered and over time fell into serious (though certainly routine relative to my environment at the time) sin, particularly in my college years and immediately after them. On some level I knew something was deeply wrong and/or missing in my life, but I had no idea what the issue was or how to figure it out. Then a close friend from college, who had never previously (to my knowledge) shown any interest in the Christian faith, took me to a weeknight presentation at a church which was an evening "seminar" on rock music and its spiritual implications. That presentation, by a former DJ of a major Chicago rock & roll radio station who had deep knowledge on that genre of music and the key people involved in it, opened my eyes to the reality of evil and of the devil. This activated my faith in God for the first time. At the end of the presentation the speaker made an altar call (an invitation to come forward and pray to receive Christ) and I immediately did so. I had no idea what to expect, in part because I'd never even heard of such a thing before. I do not know how many people went up to the altar rail and kneeled for this, but it was an impressive number, representing a significant percentage of the attendees, and the altar rail area was packed. The message had clearly reached many others just as it had reached me. The speaker led us in a prayer of repentance and acknowledgement of the Lordship of Jesus Christ, surrendering our lives to him and receiving him as savior and Lord. I distinctly remember when walking out of the church moments later, there was an immediate and powerful change in me which was obvious not only to me but also to my friend. In fact, I distinctly felt as though a thousand pounds of chains had been removed from my body, I remember feeling light as a feather, and my mind was somehow clearer than I had ever remembered it being. There were other aspects of this experience that confirmed the supernatural nature and life-changing significance of the event, along with a profound peace such as I had never before experienced. I knew at that moment I was a changed person and would henceforth be on a different track in life, though I had no idea what that would be. I had an immediate hunger to read and know scripture, attend church and be in fellowship with other Christians which grew over the ensuing weeks and months, but I really had roadmap to follow at this initial stage. I was to discover how difficult and problematic such a process could be.

A few months after this conversion experience at the age of 24, I felt the growing need for guidance from others who were more mature and informed in their faith. In the beginning of my Christian life I started to become confused about a number of major theological and spiritual issues as I encountered different perspectives on key subjects within the larger "Christian" realm. As I immersed myself in the Bible, I only became more perplexed about many important theological questions. I recognized a need for input or guidance at that point, and after praying about it, I felt led at that point to seek the counsel of a semi-retired Episcopal priest who I had once heard preach as a guest minister at a non-denominational church in my home town. He seemed unusually congenial, intelligent, energetic, educated, and I assumed highly knowledgeable on the subject matter of interest. I recall, however, being somewhat taken aback at the way he approached the relationship right from the outset. I was simply looking for someone with more experience, knowledge and hopefully wisdom in this area to answer some questions for me and provide some theological guidance. Instead, he set out to essentially "adopt" me as his "spiritual son" and expected a high degree of mental, emotional and time commitment from me. Although initially quite put-off by this approach, I gradually went along with it to a degree, as I assumed (and was being indirectly taught) that this is how God works through people in such situations— that superficial and transactional interactions such as I was allegedly looking for would not address the deeper changes that were needed. This logic made sense, and since I was developing a level of trust in him due to his unusual willingness to invest time into me, I did go along with that approach for quite some time.

Shortly after this, I attended Harvard Business School, earning my M.B.A., after which I worked for a highly-regarded Catholic charitable enterprise in New York City for two years. However, having gotten married at the end of the M.B.A. program, and having our first child one year later, I recognized a need for more career potential and joined an executive search firm where I worked for the next 3½ years before I felt called to go back to medical school and become a doctor. At that point we had 2 children and one on the way, but as ill-advised and risky as this clearly seemed, I felt this was the right decision at that time. That process went better than I had any right to expect, which I interpreted (whether rightly or wrongly) as confirmation that I had made the right move. While we were regularly attending church and I was still seeking some additional fellowship opportunities at that stage of life, in spiritual terms I was regressing (without being aware of it), and the mentoring relationship I had established previously was one major reason for that. While I believe his intentions were good, there was always a quality to this relationship and the approach to the faith that troubled me, but I wasn't able to identify the exact nature of the issues until more recent years. To be fair, some of the advice I received from that mentor was truly helpful at the time, but the overall nature and thrust of his influence was way off the mark, as I eventually came to see. In fact, it took me 24 years to reach the point of breakthrough (which itself took another few years to process) in my understanding of, and level of commitment to, God to recognize I had to completely terminate that particular relationship to eliminate a major source of profound compromise in my spiritual life. Directly related to this, I also came to recognize that I also needed to leave the Episcopal church (where I had been going in recent years and most of my post-conversion and all of my pre-conversion life) and find a church which was faithfully and consistently committed to the authority and inerrancy of the word of God. This obviously involved a radical departure from all that was familiar to me (religiously) up to then. But here is the point of this whole story: *my breakthrough came unequivocally as a result of my investing significant time in reading the Bible, praying a lot, and eventually surrendering to the written and inward revelation of God.*

This process brought me to the overwhelming recognition that the Bible is God's supernaturally inspired and crafted word to us that is valid and universally applicable for all people and all time. When I recognized that and the clear and, frankly, glaring discrepancies between the word of God and many important perspectives of this well-intentioned mentor/priest, it became obvious I could not continue to participate in a mentoring relationship with someone who, however brilliant and earnest he may have been, was at significant variance with the overall perspective presented by the word of God, especially on itself as definitive truth. The core problem was this: he had been taught, and embraced, a perspective on the Bible that it is an allegedly imperfect product of flawed human beings and that much of the most important information presented in it was either "metaphorical," "allegorical" or influenced by (and by implication, applicable only to) the prevailing culture of that time and place. In other words, he believed the Bible contained much wisdom but was not the ultimate source of all truth— rather, that we needed to evaluate its teachings and where it did not make sense or seem applicable to the current time and place in which we live, to reject it as flawed and limited for a different standard. That standard was, by definition, to be determined by us, and by the collective "wisdom" of whatever group we might find most congenial theologically. It became clear to me that he fell right into the heart of theological liberalism which, as previously described, is a fundamentally different approach to the Bible than the one I have been advocating in this book. Nevertheless, this is actually the predominant perspective on the Bible held by most major or "name brand" seminaries (such as Harvard Divinity and Yale Divinity Schools, both of which I am well acquainted with, and Union Theological Seminary in New York City, whose current president admitted in an interview in the New York Times she does not believe in the virgin birth or resurrection of Jesus Christ) and church denominations in the U.S. today. Thankfully, however, there are still many seminaries and churches that agree completely with, and are fully committed to, the view of scripture I have been presenting and are bold and unapologetic in saying so since the issue is of the foremost importance. In sheer numbers, however, the former vastly eclipse the latter in the United States, and the massive and widespread effects on our churches and our culture have been devastating and are far-reaching. Schleiermacher would be proud of the American seminary and church scene today! But the real question is this: is God pleased with this migration away from, and ultimately rejection of, biblical authority? Is he pleased when those of us who have had ample exposure to scripture teach that the Bible is wrong on a number of extremely important subjects, yet act as though we revere it—and God? There is a great deal of scripture which makes it clear that God is not pleased with such behavior and that it represents rebellion against God himself. Furthermore, scripture testifies throughout that it is the very word of God which is by definition timeless and authoritative in every age, place, people group and circumstance. I recognize that this perspective can only be reached by faith given the wide-reaching implications, but if it is in fact true, then it would only be foolishness to continue to reject—in part or in whole—the unique, complete, definitive and final written revelation of God.

Regarding my own experience in this regard, ending that mentoring relationship and the change in church affiliation were necessary and of paramount importance in the process of my spiritual growth and liberation (in addition to the immersion in the Bible and prayer which made such liberation possible). The positive impact of these changes on my life personally as well as that of my marriage and my relationships with my children and family, friends, colleagues and patients is clear, at least to me, though admittedly there is still plenty of work to do to get all aspects of my life in good order. Breaking off a long and significant relationship is difficult, and often painful and disruptive, but such decisions about some longstanding relationships and affiliations will be necessary for those who wish to be a rock and to be as unencumbered as possible by values and perspectives that are flawed or otherwise counterproductive. It was, very simply, the Bible and the help of the Holy Spirit that eventually though decisively brought me to the point of my own personal liberation from the tyranny of warped, man-made, and in some cases demon-inspired doctrines. Only after making those changes did I begin to experience the true freedom made possible in Christ and the fruits of the Holy Spirit referenced above. Freedom from fear of man. Freedom from being manipulable through guilt or shame. Freedom from false doctrines that undermine the authority of God and scriptures, regardless of the credentials of anyone teaching them. Freedom from the false urgency of insignificant matters according to worldly values. Freedom from enslavement to the opinions or acceptance of others. Freedom from greed, lust, and other uncontrolled natural appetites that can destroy you. Freedom even from the threat of death—the ultimate adversary and nemesis of all people. Ultimately, such comprehensive freedom bestows a gift which many people would give everything they own to have, or would do anything, no matter how arduous, to achieve: deep, durable inner peace regardless of externals. Many authors, spiritual teachers and TV personalities (such as Oprah as discussed above) go to great lengths to teach people how to achieve such peace, but without a correct roadmap and paradigm for spiritual reality, such pursuits are nothing but human efforts based on human wisdom which fall far short of the truth on this matter. And that truth was perfectly expressed by Jesus Christ himself when he said, "*My peace I give you. Not as the world gives you.*" (John 14:27) So based on just these benefits alone, it should be clear how ill-advised it would be to reject the full divine inspiration and authority of the Bible—yet the majority of people in the theological realms these days seem to do just that.

To sum my little personal story up, just as Martin Luther did his own epic and world-changing story: "The Word did it all!" That is not an overstatement, though without the assistance of the Holy Spirit and ample prayer, we would not only fail to understand but we would continue to resist the truth presented in the Bible. The role of the Word, the Bible, was certainly critical, and what it did for me and innumerable people throughout history, it can do for you, if you are truly seeking God and willing to hear what He has to tell you.

I need to put all this in perspective. During those many years where I was not functioning as a "rock" to my family, due to the combination of the relentless pursuit of worldly success and accomplishments and my shortcomings in the character qualities, worldview and value set which are the subject of this book, my family unfortunately did suffer, and the harm was real. At the time what little of it I was aware of seemed to be unavoidable "collateral damage" from life in this world. I now know it does not have to be that way. In the latter years, the seriousness of the costs to myself and others of failing to be the rock I should have been, particularly in terms of spiritual leadership but also in other ways, has become clear. This recognition is so weighty to me that I would readily give up everything for which I've worked and striven so hard most of my life if I could go back and change the way I performed on the most important responsibilities and functions of my life. However, by the grace of God and guided by his word, having engaged with the Rock Himself, with abundant prayer and fellowship being instrumental in that process for a number of years now, it is all gradually being reoriented, reordered, redeemed, restored and healed. The good—actually amazing—news is that even in the later stages of life, it is still possible to turn it all around in ways we think are impossible, if we are willing to embrace the perspective of Matthew 7:24-27 and seek and accept God's assistance in doing so. This is no easy quick fix but rather a fundamental change in our paradigm of life and the way in which we live it out.

My point here is to recognize the supreme importance of being properly grounded and having a correct paradigm of reality as well as availing yourself of the very present and real help of God. When we go it alone and operate out of our own natural thinking, relying on our own strength, intelligence and judgment, we will always fall short of our potential, as well fail to respond to God's call on our lives, particularly in those most critical areas of life such as marriage and parenthood. Wherever you are spiritually or whatever your phase of life, if you lay hold of this opportunity and diligently and consistently pursue your relationship with God through the Bible, prayer and fellowship with other believers, you *will* see the substance we are speaking of form within yourself and will come to understand life and your assignments in it from a correct (and God-centered) perspective.

Ask, and it will be given to you; seek and you will find; knock and it will be opened to you. For everyone who asks receives, and the one who seeks finds, and to the one who knocks it will be opened. (Matthew 7:7-8)

Questions for reflection:

1. What are your key and non-negotiable criteria for a church in which to fellowship and cultivate deep connections with the body of Christ?

2. Is it possible for a church which rejects important biblical standards and values to be fully faithful to God, and therefore a place you would consider making your own church?

3.   Have you ever faced a major dilemma involving the authority of scripture in your life, and if so, how was that dilemma resolved?

4.   Do you agree with the following verse, and if so, are you ready to live it out?

But seek first the kingdom of God and his righteousness, and all these things will be added to you. (Matthew 6:33)

Final Thoughts

We human beings are by nature fallible, fickle, and have a short (in the larger perspective) and uncertain lifespan. Our lives are characterized by weakness and shortcomings that to varying degrees lead to failure in the most important areas of life and real harm to ourselves, our loved ones, and the world. On top of this, we live in a world where chaos, confusion and disruption are a given. We are so inherently unstable and unreliable that we are in great need of a stabilizing force based on reliable and eternal truth that does not change or fail under the most difficult, chaotic or fearful circumstances. The internal and personal fallibility is the main issue we must address. While being a rock should have positive effects on those in our immediate circle of influence, our outlook (unlike a number of other prevailing ideologies) is not to change the world as a whole or to solve all its problems, but to be faithful and effective in all our core responsibilities and relationships.

Our universal response, however, to our inadequacy, instability and sense of insignificance is to turn to ideologies, causes, relationships, groups, institutions, substances or pursuits that provide us a sense of being part of something bigger and better than ourselves, which may also provide a false sense of transcendence and significance. Unfortunately, these will all fail us at the point of greatest need. The greater truth is that there is an infinitely stable, reliable, trustworthy, all-sufficient, willing and benevolent Rock we can actually "attach" to, thereby introducing a profoundly durable and powerful stability, groundedness and reliability into our lives. Far more than that, as great as that is, are all the riches of the good gifts and purposes God has for you and me specifically. Although we are, in our natural state, rebels from the reign and rule of God, by his grace and mercy alone we can be restored to harmonious fellowship with God which is a dynamic reality ordering our thoughts, priorities and actions and leading to untold blessing on us and those about whom we care most. This occurs through a recognition of the Lordship of Jesus Christ and our fallen and sinful condition before him, followed by genuine repentance and unreserved acceptance of him as Lord of our life, resulting in total forgiveness and regeneration unto new life which we come to find is also eternal. I have discovered, and consider to be abundantly shown, this truth and the reality of this principle in my life, and I can confidently say that the same truth and opportunity applies to you. The written revelation of God, which I (and many millions of people throughout the world) recognize as the 66 books of the Old and New Testaments, provides the only definitive, reliable, validated, living, active, and unchanging truth as revealed in writing by God the Holy Spirit through his faithful servants, whose imperfection has not corrupted this written revelation in any significant way. There simply is no other such definitive, complete and perfect written revelation of the one and only living God and His remarkable relationship with His people over millennia. The Bible is entirely in a class of its own, and once we come to terms with that fact, which requires us (at least it did for me!) to humble ourselves in obedience to God's expressly revealed word and to stop arguing with it, analyzing it for flaws, doubting and resisting it, or believing (mostly on account of ignorance of it) untrue but prevalent errors about the Bible, God will bless you with increasing faith, wisdom, stability, peace and soundness of mind, purity of heart, and harmony with God, a blessed condition that takes on eternal significance and has impact throughout generations to come. God is a good, good Father to his people, the resources he provides to help you are infinite, and He freely gives everything needed and beneficial to those who ask for them. However, I urge you not to simply take my word for it, as that may have little lasting impact, but to investigate this yourselves to determine the validity of this claim. You will not be disappointed. Coming to a full (as full as possible in this life) understanding of the unique and great gift that the Bible is may be likened to the parable spoken by Jesus regarding the infinite value of the Kingdom of God: *Again, the Kingdom of heaven is like a merchant in search of fine pearls who, on finding one pearl of great value, went and sold all that he had and bought it.* (Matthew 13:45-46)

The process of becoming "a rock" is a delicate one. Because of the changes required of us, it may, and at times probably will, be disruptive even in some key areas of life including habits, relationships and affiliations or avocations. If we take on a level of substance and stability that is unusual in the world, even if that is what "normal" is actually supposed to look like, it tends to put us at odds at times with people, since many of the people in our lives may not embrace this perspective (at least fully) because it involves a specific revealed knowledge of the true identity, nature, and will of the God of the universe. This in turn has comprehensive implications for our paradigm of life. There may very well come moments of crisis in our lives as a result of standing firmly for, and on, this truth. But as the Bible says, the connection to God through Christ and the comfort, peace, wisdom and other benefits that are given us by the Holy Spirit and the word of God are worth far more than all that the world (or people) can possibly offer in the final analysis. In addition, living our lives being guided by the wisdom of the people around us and the conventional wisdom of our culture coming through from multiple sources every day, is not really living at all, whereas being grounded on and connected to the Rock is life and freedom indeed.

May we be willing to pay the price to personally and eternally lay hold of the Kingdom of heaven, the key to which is simply having a personal and real relationship with the living God through deeply knowing and diligently reading the Bible daily, making it our lifeblood, engraving it on our hearts and minds, so we may build the house of our lives on the only sound foundation, the Rock, rejoicing in this remarkably great gift God has given all people for their salvation and blessing, and for his glory, honor and praise.

Trust in the Lord forever, for the Lord God is an everlasting rock. (Isaiah 30:29)

Acknowledgements

There were a number of individuals who provided important help and feedback in the process of writing and producing this book. Each of the following special people sacrificed significant time to provide me with their valuable input, and I am deeply thankful and greatly indebted to them all: the Rev. Dr. Peter Jones, Rev. Dr. Nathan Hart, the Hon. Gregory Slayton, Rev. John Rankin, Rev. Thomas Oates, David Kupelian, Jay Pasqualoni, Sheri Pasqualoni, Glen Ramsteck, Andrew Allis, and Dr. Jeffrey Romine. I also want to specifically thank Bill Thomson for his extraordinary talent, consummate professionalism, and world class artistry with which he was able to take my basic vision for the cover art and to capture and execute it so perfectly as a blessing to the readers. Finally, I want to thank my beloved wife, Joanne, and our four amazing children, Chase, Brynn, Carter and Will, for their patience, support, encouragement and love—you are my greatest treasure and prize in this life.

About the Author

Dr. Reynolds is a nephrologist in full-time clinical practice in a multispecialty group private practice in Connecticut. He has been married for 32 years and is blessed with four wonderful children. Prior to undergoing medical training he worked in the nonprofit and business worlds. His life experience and providential factors have led him on a journey of faith which serves as the inspiration for this book. He is board certified in nephrology and is a member of the American Society of Nephrology. He is an actively involved member of his local church, a Board member of the Fellowship of Fathers Foundation, and a supporter a number of Christian and missionary enterprises. He earned his MD with honors from Yale School of Medicine, and his MBA from Harvard Business School. Dr. Reynolds invites his readers to contact him with any questions at jtreynoldsmd@gmail.com